THE
COMPLETE
DR. SALK

*An A-to-Z Guide to
Raising Your Child*

THE COMPLETE DR. SALK

An A-to-Z Guide to Raising Your Child

LEE SALK

Clinical Professor of Psychology in Psychiatry
and Clinical Professor of Pediatrics
The New York Hospital—Cornell Medical Center

World Almanac Publications
New York, New York

First published in paperback in 1984.

Newspaper Enterprise Association ISBN   0-911818-49-9

Ballantine Books ISBN   0-345-31651-7

Library of Congress   83-051723

A hardcover edition of this book was originally published by NAL
Books, a division of New American Library.

Printed in the United States of America

World Almanac Publications
Newspaper Enterprise Association, Inc.
A Division of United Media Enterprises, Inc.
A Scripps-Howard Company
200 Park Avenue
New York, NY 10166

10 9 8 7 6 5 4 3 2 1

I dedicate this book to all loving parents everywhere who offer kindness, compassion, and understanding to their children. And to all non-parents who give children a feeling of recognition and importance.

My appreciation to Randi Londer for her superb contribution to researching and editing this book.

And to my editor, June Foley, whose deep sensitivity to my philosophy and style of communication, along with her sensitivity as a parent and a warm human being, made working on this book a marvelous experience.

THE COMPLETE DR. SALK

An A-to-Z Guide to Raising Your Child

INTRODUCTION

Family life has changed radically, decade to decade, since the turn of the century. Recent trends include a majority of mothers—and 45, percent of mothers of preschool children—working outside the home; a growing percentage of women delaying childbirth until they are in their thirties and have completed their education and established themselves in a career; a growing percentage of children being raised in a single-parent household, most of these headed by a woman; and a growing involvement of fathers in childrearing, by taking on the primary responsibility for their children, by becoming more involved with their children even though they are in their mothers' "custody," or by assuming greater responsibility for and involvement with their children within a two-parent household.

The changes are now accelerating at a rapid rate. It is almost impossible to predict what the future will bring. But despite the uncertainties, some elements of life remain the same. Human development is still influenced by genetics, physiology, and experience. A mutually satisfying relationship as a baby with at least one parent is still the foundation of the ability to love as an adult. The parents' guidance in developing a child's ability to cope with life's stresses independently, to plan ahead, and to postpone immediate satisfaction for greater satisfaction later is still the foundation of the ability to learn and eventually to find one's life's work.

In my many years as a practicing psychologist I have treated every conceivable problem, and have gained a great deal of insight into the factors that contribute to emotional disorders, both large and small.

I have been profoundly impressed with how much easier it is to *prevent* emotional ills in infancy and early childhood than it is to treat them later in life.

That is the reason for this book. It provides parents, in a concise, readable form, with the knowledge I have gained, in the hope that parents can avoid some of the causes of emotional problems in their children and can provide their children with the greatest possible degree of healthy development in terms of the child's own potential.

This is a book for parents of children of all ages. It can be used as a reference when specific questions or difficulties arise. But it can also be read straight through as a primer on child-rearing.

A child's development from birth to maturity goes through a series of developmental processes. We can think of this as a series of critical challenges. The ages vary, but the order is the same for everyone. How well each challenge is met is determined partly by how well earlier challenges were met, and this in turn determines how successfully the next stage will be met. For instance, if an infant's first needs for food and comfort, contact and stimulation, are gratified, he develops a sense of trust that becomes the basis for learning to get around on his own, away from his mother or father—whoever the primary caretaker is—at a later point in childhood.

At the first stage in a child's development, parents need to hold, hug, cuddle, play with, sing to, and talk to their child. They need to provide things for their child to look at, listen to, smell, touch, and taste. They need to come when their child cries. It is essential that the infant establish a positive and trusting relationship with at least one other human being, so that he comes to view human contact as rewarding.

Sometime in the second year, when the baby can move around on his own and interact with more of his surroundings, parents need to set limits on his behavior, and to provide learning experiences by encouraging his awareness of his environment.

During the first school years the child takes his initial tentative steps outside the home circle into friendships with other children, and he learns to manipulate abstract symbols in order to read, write, think logically, and solve problems effectively. In order to learn during this stage, the child needs to have successfully completed the first two stages. That is, he needs to have developed trust, so that he believes it is worthwhile to please others, including his teacher; and he needs to have developed self-control, so that he refrains from acting on impulse. This is the groundwork that makes it possible for him to acquire the appropriate social behavior and intellectual skills. These in turn will help him through the essential process of his later school years, which is establishing his own identity as an individual.

Avoiding emotional disturbance and encouraging the child's fullest development depends on understanding what the essential goal of each developmental process is, and what general conditions will help him meet it in order to prepare him for the next stage. Cut-and-dried answers to questions like, "When should you wean a baby?" are hit-and-miss solutions at best. It's much more helpful for parents to have an idea of the main goals of each stage of development. Parents can then think about those goals in relation to their individual child and their own particular circumstances.

This book attempts to help parents facilitate their children's fullest development. Which is not to say that this book, or any book, or anything *else,* makes parenthood easy. Taking on parenthood means taking on an enormous commitment and a tremendous responsibility. There is no simple how-to guide. Human behavior cannot be reduced to a series of recipes, or lists of do's and don't's. There is absolutely no way a parent can get from one day to the next without experiencing problems. There's no such thing as having family responsibilities without having difficulties. Most parents at some time or another feel absolutely overwhelmed. Not only is parenthood difficult, but it is largely unrewarded by the rest of society. Often it seems as though children are regarded as a nuisance, and parenthood as a bother.

Nevertheless, I believe that being a parent is the most important role a human being can assume. I have personally put my role as the parent of two children before everything else. My professional life has been organized to provide the flexibility necessary for my children to be primary.

I myself am convinced that being a good parent is the most challenging and the most meaningful of life's experiences. It is my hope that this book can help more people experience the unique joy and pride of parenthood by helping their children fulfill their potential as human beings who are able to learn, love, and work—and eventually become good parents themselves.

A

ACCEPTANCE
(SEE ALSO *Affection, Love, Praise, Rejection*)

It seems to me that there is nothing more valuable and basic to a parent-child relationship than acceptance, love, and affection. These feelings sensitize a child to other people and provide a firm foundation for successful relationships in the future. Acceptance and affection help a child understand that rewards come from human interaction, which can counteract the greed, hostility, and destructiveness in the world. A child needs to feel that you accept her as a person, unconditionally. This does not mean that you necessarily condone her behavior in all circumstances. However, she should feel that she is accepted by you and will continue to be accepted by you, regardless of her behavior.

The opposite of acceptance, of course, is rejection. Typically, a child will feel rejected when her mother leaves her to go off to the hospital, only to return with a new baby. I remember a three-year-old whose parents presented her with a new baby brother; shortly afterward the child disobeyed her mother and was reprimanded. The child burst into tears and asked, "Mommy, are you going to give me back to the hospital?" She felt doubly rejected—because she felt the new baby had taken her place, and because her mother became angry. If this sort of thing happens, you can pick up your child, hold her, and tell her, "Look, I love you, but I'm angry right now."

It's important to give adolescents a feeling of acceptance, even though they're older and more independent, and may be behaving in ways that you can't condone. The alienation of adolescents who do not feel accepted within their families sometimes leads them to seek acceptance in gangs or cults as substitute families, or to become isolated "loners." Be sure your teenager understands that even though her haircut or wardrobe are not those you would choose for yourself, even though her musical preference gives you a headache and her political views are the opposite of your own, you respect her individuality and accept her without condition.

ACCIDENT PRONE
(SEE ALSO *Adolescence, Neurological Disturbances, Neurosis*)

Some children have frequent accidents. This can occur simply because of what is considered clumsiness, or poor motor coordination. In most instances this improves with time as a child's muscle coordination develops. In addition, some children are the "absent-minded professor" type; their minds are miles away from wherever their bodies happen to be. And an adolescent growth spurt can make a youngster temporarily awkward, and thus accident prone. As a teenager, my son Eric bumped into doorways so often that he finally explained, "I've grown so fast, and there's so much more of me than there used to be, that I just haven't gotten used to going through doors at this height."

Some children who have frequent accidents may have a neurological disorder or a form of epilepsy that causes them to lose consciousness momentarily. Other neurological disorders can cause a child to simply collapse but regain muscle control in a matter of seconds. This is not a problem to be diagnosed by parents themselves. The symptoms of frequent accidents or falling should be a warning sign that your child needs to be seen by a pediatric neurologist.

In some instances accident proneness is caused by emotional factors. When a person harbors a great deal of hostility and anger, or feels caught in a double bind (damned if he does and damned if he doesn't), the result can be some form of aggression turned toward himself. In a sense it's a way of venting pent-up emotions that can't be resolved in a more direct manner. While this kind of disorder is not frequently found in children, the symptoms warrant professional attention. Even if you suspect that the problem is caused by emotional factors, it is still wise to investigate with a neurologist the possibility that some nervous system disorder is causing poor coordination or occasional lapses of consciousness.

ADOLESCENCE

(SEE ALSO *Acceptance, Accident Prone, Alcohol and Drug Abuse Among Teenagers, Ambivalence, Anorexia Nervosa, Approval, Boredom, Bossiness, Dating, Defiance, Depression, Disrespect, Drinking, Drugs, Friends, Gang, Hero Worship, Independence, Individuality, Juvenile Delinquency, Laziness, Listening, Lying, Masturbation, Messiness, Model Child, Obscenity, Overprotectiveness, Pornography, Reasoning, Rebellion, Regression, Rejection, Religion, Responsibility, Sex Education, Sexual Experiences, Schizophrenia, School, Self-Esteem, Smoking, Stuttering, Television, Video Games, Withdrawn Child*)

The adolescent is experiencing the most rapid growth and the greatest changes in her life except for her first year. The physical changes during adolescence are enormous; and in our culture, the emotional turmoil during this period is often enormous as well. For every teenager whose identity unfolds as easily, gracefully, and inevitably as a bud into a blossom, there are several who shoot up as suddenly and awkwardly as weeds.

If your teenager behaves as though she's unbalanced, don't be surprised. She *is* unbalanced. She has one foot in childhood and the other in adulthood. She wonders who she is.

Her parents may also wonder who she is. The parents of a teenager often feel as if their household had been taken over by a stranger, and a hostile one at that. Where is their sweet little girl? Simply, she is growing up. She is struggling to become herself, her own person. This means that parents must change their perception of their teenager as a "little girl" and allow her the freedom and independence that will enable her to further develop the resources that she will need to assume her place in the world as an adult. Parents should bear in mind that as part of this process, she may demand to do things her own way, then shift her opinions from one extreme to another, and will almost certainly make mistakes.

At this stage of life, as at every stage, parents should be aware of what their youngster is experiencing. If they recognize that growth, change, unpredictability are all a normal part of adolescent development in our culture, they can continue to help their daughter meet the challenge of this stage of development in the same way they helped her meet earlier challenges.

The parents of adolescents should continue to be firm, and at the same time warm and comforting, thus meeting their teenager's need for both limits and protection. At the same time, they can offer her the flexibility and freedom she needs to learn to make her own decisions, test her own limits, and profit from her own mistakes.

I believe that a great deal of adolescent rebellion is caused by the inability of parents and other adults to accept what is part of normal development. When young people become physically larger and begin to mature sexually, they understandably want to act in more of the ways that our culture considers "adult." Often, parents who are reluctant to see their "babies" grow up consciously or unconsciously hold them back. This is frustrating, embarrassing, and painful to the young people involved.

If we insist that adolescents follow our orders and accept our values, we can be sure that they will rebel against us. In fact, this is true not only for adolescents but in any other situation in life when people attempt to exercise power over others. When children are younger, parents are larger, stronger, and better able to control the behavior of their children; but as children grow, parents no longer have this power.

Many parents worry that if they allow their teenagers too much freedom and flexibility, they will hurt themselves. For this reason, many parents continue to tell their teenagers what do do, instead of allowing them to work things out for themselves. But the only way that teenagers—or anyone else—can learn is by doing things themselves, and even by making mistakes.

Adolescence is a time of growth and change, but it is not *necessarily* a time of constant conflict between parents and teenagers; the conflict can be diminished if parents continue to encourage their children to develop their own talents, skills, and resources to become independent individuals who are able to cope with the world on their own. Happily, parents can do so trusting that if they have had a basically open, warm, and satisfying relationship with their children up to adolescence, that relationship should reassert itself in time.

ADOPTION

I have great admiration for people who adopt children. There are so many children in the world who desperately need love and care that it is gratifying to know that people will go through complex and time-consuming procedures to make their homes and their lives available to children.

If you adopt a newborn, I recommend that you treat him just like your natural-born child. You may find it somewhat difficult to get used to the child, but in fact your experience is not much different from that of natural parents at the time their child is born.

Whenever the time seems natural and right, or whenever the subject comes up, you should give your child a frank and uncomplicated explanation of his adoption. You should be relaxed and open, emphasizing how much you wanted a child, and what a happy event your child's adoption was for you. If your child asks you whether you are his "real" parent, you might explain that there are two ways parents can have children—either biologically or by adopting. Make it clear that the person in whose body the child grew need not be more significant than the person who is actually raising the child. If your child is worried that his biological parents didn't want him, you might acknowledge that allowing him to be adopted was almost certainly a very difficult decision, and was made out of love for the child and concern for his welfare. Your child's curiosity is natural, and doesn't mean that he is dissatisfied with you. Allow your child to ask questions, and to express any of his feelings about being adopted. For some children, the questioning process will be continuous. Some children may want to know different things at different

9

times: "Where did you get me?" "Did you know my other mother and father?"

Some children may repeat the same questions and listen to the same answers again and again: "Why did my mother give me away?" Be truthful. If you lie or evade the truth, your child may sense this and may conclude that there is something wrong or bad about adoption—or even about himself. Or he may learn the truth from someone else and may feel betrayed.

Choosing to adopt an older child means a different set of challenges and a different attitude, perhaps, about what you hope to achieve as a parent. If you mean to mold an older child to follow your ways, to adopt your values, and to show love, appreciation, and devotion to you at all times, you are probably in for a disappointment. If, however, you wish to provide a child with a home and an opportunity to develop his own resources and a sense of self-esteem, you stand a good chance of becoming a successful parent, rearing a happy and healthy child.

You must be realistic in your expectations and recognize that older children have already had many learning experiences, perhaps under circumstances very different from those in your own life. As a result, the child's attitudes, feelings, and values may be quite unlike yours. This does not mean that adopting an older child is a bad or even necessarily a questionable idea. It simply calls for more understanding and patience on your part and a greater effort to accept the individuality of that child. As a general rule, it is probably easier if the child you adopt *is* young—but some of the most challenging experiences in life are the most fulfilling.

ADVICE FROM OUTSIDERS

New parents often receive plenty of unsolicited advice from relatives, friends, and even strangers on how to care for their new baby. While all these people mean well, they are often dead wrong.

Right after a woman gives birth, her emotions can be fragile; she may be highly vulnerable to believing anything she hears from others and believing she is wrong. Visitors often recount their experience as gospel, implying that they have more experience and therefore that they know best. I think such people are really envious of the new mother and unconsciously want to undermine the pleasure she is having with her child. Their attitude is what I would call "anti-parent." Here is an illustration of what I mean: When a mother feeds her newborn for the first time and notices her infant looking straight into her face while suckling the breast or the bottle, that new mother experiences a warm, excited feeling. The exhilarated mother, usually wanting to share her happiness at this moment, calls someone over and says, "See, my baby is looking at me!" Often it is a professional who, in an officious or detached manner, simply says, "Not possible. Your baby can't see yet." Then the dismayed parent is told that a baby can't see until two weeks, or three weeks, or four weeks, or six weeks of age, depending on where the professional was trained. But the fact is that a newborn baby does see and does tend to look directly into the face of the person who is feeding her. This is erroneous advice that contradicts what the mother has just experienced. Worse, the advice tended to debase the capabilities of a newborn baby and minimize the importance of the warm and dramatic experience the mother just had. This kind of unfounded advice detracts from the pleasure you will get from your infant. That's why I call it "anti-parent." Why would a newborn look a mother straight in the face immediately upon suckling the breast or bottle if the mother's face was not an object of importance? Why doesn't the baby look elsewhere? This experience tells me that a baby is not only capable of seeing, but is capable of associating his mother's face with the pleasure that is about to take place in the feeding process.

Another gratifying moment for new parents is when their baby first smiles. Generally, an excited parent turns to some professional and says, "Look! My baby is smiling!" More often than not, the professional answers, "No, no. That's not a smile. That's gas." I think this is ridiculous. Gas doesn't make me smile and I am sure it doesn't make you smile. Neither does it make a baby smile. Why should gas cause a smile any more than a smile cause gas? I think the notion that gas makes a baby smile developed a long time ago when some baby smiled and coincidentally passed gas at the very same moment. Some professional who was observing immediately concluded that the gas caused a smile. The observation was then transmitted as gospel. Many unfounded bits of information have been accumulated and passed on in this way.

I am often asked how parents can be sure that their pediatrician is giving them good advice about their child's behavior and their emotional reactions to the child's behavior. The answer is that it's very hard to be sure. Although there seems to be more and more interest in increasing pediatric training in child-rearing practices, I don't think parents can take it for granted that all pediatricians are well-versed in child psychology. You should be wary of pediatrians who tend to undermine your confidence, downgrade your natural tendencies, give advice without explaining the basis for their advice, or imply that you are neurotic.

A lot of unsound advice is transmitted not only by friends and professionals, but by the parents of new parents as well. These are the very people who should be most supportive of you and your offspring. But many new grandparents find it difficult to think of their child, who is also now a parent, as anything but a youngster who is not yet mature enough to undertake the responsibilities of parenthood. The grandparents think their child is not sufficiently knowledgeable to be a parent unless given all kinds of advice. Unless you have achieved a certain degree of independence from your parents, it is extremely hard to resist this kind of pressure. Nevertheless, if you have not gotten your parents to recognize and accept your individuality, this is the time to insist they do. If you do not, it will be extremely hard for you to raise your own child with a sense of self-confidence and for your own child to trust and respect you as an individual.

I do not mean that grandparents' advice should always be ignored, but I do think it is important that new parents acknowledge their own natural tendencies and follow them.

AFFECTION
(SEE ALSO *Acceptance, Love, Love-Hate Relationships*)

Parental affection helps a child feel important in the life of the parent. Through demonstrative affection—hugs, kisses, and physical contact—children can feel your warmth and love. These gestures, without feeling, rarely fool a child into believing you are sincere. Being demonstratively loving to a child one moment and rejecting him the next, without any rational basis, leaves a child anxious and fearful of losing your love. I'm not suggesting that you never show anger or annoyance; I'm simply pointing out that affection should be consistent. It's confusing to be kissed and hugged one minute and rejected the next. While there are cultural differences that account for some people's greater emphasis on physical affection, there is a clear need on the part of babies and young children to be touched and held, fondled, kissed, and cuddled. Many children enjoy jumping into their parents' bed in the morning and snuggling with them cozily. I can't think of anything more wonderful. It's important, too, for children to see their parents demonstrate affection toward one another, even though children may experience some moments of jealousy. As adults, many of us can still vividly recall an episode in our youth when our parents were warm and tender to one another; we remember the warm and happy feeling it gave us; we remain touched by their love.

AGGRESSION
(SEE ALSO *Anger, Arguments Between Parents, Day Care, Defiance, Discipline and Punishment, Head Banging, Sibling, Television, Temper Tantrums, Video Games*)

Very young children—around two to three years old—often behave aggressively toward other children. They are not yet developmentally mature enough to play "with" one another in a truly cooperative way; instead, they merely play alongside one another in what is called "parallel play." At this age, children tend to simply grab things that they want from one another. They are very crude indeed in the expression of their feelings, and it's not uncommon for them to be hostile without the least bit of remorse. When aggression occurs, I think it is important for you to demonstrate that you are annoyed or angry about such behavior, and to remove the child from the play situation if he becomes destructive. It is impossible to reason with two-year-olds and have them understand the implications of the aggression. They will respond more to your emotional reaction than to attempts to explain why such behavior is unacceptable. You must clearly *show* your child by your facial expression and your tone of voice that aggression is unacceptable. Otherwise, your child will never develop a repentant attitude.

It is important for you to set limits on what is acceptable behavior and what is not. You will have to reaffirm these limits periodically—and prepare yourself for the fact that, at times, your child will ignore them. The essential point is to be consistent and let your child know that if he continues to do these things you prohibit, you will have to punish him. If your punishment is appropriate and not overly severe, and comes within the context of a warm and loving relationship, he will begin to incorporate your values into his life, and, in this way, begin to develop internal controls over his own behavior.

Aggression, for the most part, comes from frustration. Parents who are very strict and prohibitive with their children can cause such a buildup of frustration that these children become very angry and aggressive and displace it onto other children or the community. It's important for children to have a chance to vent their frustration, anger, and hostility in socially acceptable ways, in order to avoid the buildup of tension that can lead to severe outbursts of rage. If children are encouraged to talk out their anger there is less likelihood of aggression in their relationships with others.

Some aggression in childhood is the direct result of parents who are overly aggressive themselves and encourage their children in this direction. Children are sometimes told by parents to "fight it out." I totally disagree with this. It is far better for the child to learn how to "talk it out," to verbalize his problems and his feelings, and to work at arriving at constructive solutions.

Sometimes a very impulsive child hits before he thinks. You might suggest to such a child that he try to control himself by counting to ten first or by saying to himself, "Stop and think." Of course, children often imitate the violence they see on TV and in movies, so I think it is wise to reduce their exposure to aggressive acts in movies or on TV. At the same time, children need more positive role models. They need to learn from their parents' examples, that people can express their angry feelings with words, and can arrive at constructive solutions to their problems.

ALCOHOL AND DRUG ABUSE AMONG TEENAGERS
(SEE ALSO *Adolescence, Drinking, Independence, Individuality, Smoking*)

There's hardly one parent among us who has not at some time been concerned about the possibility that his or her own child is engaging in alcohol or drug abuse later in life. Many, if not most, teenagers experiment with drinking liquor and smoking marijuana. But as far as abuse is concerned, it is important for parents to know that this sort of behavior is not something that starts in adolescence. It has its roots in early childhood and manifests itself later on.

Teenagers sample alcohol and drugs for a number of reasons. They are available, sometimes even on school playgrounds. Often peer pressure is involved. Some youngsters just want to experiment, either out of curiosity, or a mild sort of rebellion and the thrill of breaking rules and ignoring the law. Some youngsters who feel awkward socially or sexually use alcohol or drugs to bolster their self-confidence.

However, people who engage in alcohol and drug abuse are doing something self-destructive. No one who has self-esteem does such things. Children who have been raised to feel important in the lives of their parents feel that their thoughts and feelings matter. Children who have been given an opportunity to express themselves and to participate in family decisions feel sufficiently important to avoid doing anything self-destructive. It's essential that parents recognize this.

The more honest you are with your children as they grow up and the more responsive you are to their ideas—even if you don't necessarily agree with them—the more they feel you accept their individuality. And this acceptance contributes heavily to the development of the kind of person who is strong enough to turn away from alcohol and drugs.

The children of parents who have lied, broken promises, and otherwise given them reason to distrust them, will not believe anything their parents tell them, including their warnings against alcohol and drugs.

In essence, the best way to prevent alcohol and drug abuse later on is by being an honest parent, a parent who is responsive to a child's needs and feelings and ideas, a parent who is respectful of a child and makes the child feel truly important to the parent and the family.

Everyone needs to feel satisfaction from the completion of tasks. They need to gain a sense of accomplishment that comes from such completion. If a child has never gotten that satisfaction, because no one has ever shown a sense of pride in his accomplishments, he fails to learn to work. He then expects immediate gratification rather than expecting to work toward long-range goals, which are ultimately more fulfilling. If a child has never gotten "high" on achievement, he is prone to seeking it out chemically through drugs and alcohol.

Clearly, the time to tackle alcohol and drug abuse is from the beginning of your child's life; and the way to do so is by encouraging your child's sense of self-esteem and importance. If he feels good enough about himself, his family, and his future, he will not hurt himself by indulging in alcohol and drug abuse.

ALLOWANCE
(SEE ALSO *Family, Independence, Responsibility, Toilet Training*)

I think children should be given allowances to help them develop a sense of responsibility about money. There is no specific age I can recommend for starting a child on an allowance because so many factors are involved. You should base your decision on your own economic situation and the general standards of the community in which you live.

It's important for children to know that they can count on receiving a set amount of money, paid to them regularly, because it gives them the opportunity to plan ahead for purchases, and perhaps even to learn how to save their money by putting part of each allowance into the bank.

Parents who withhold all or part of a child's allowance as punishment for misbehavior often get fast, positive results. However, I believe that the long-term losses resulting from this kind of punishment are more significant than the immediate benefits. By withholding allowances for misbehavior or giving financial bonuses for "good" behavior, the child begins to associate money with love and acceptance, and I don't believe money should be used in this way. It's far more effective in the long run if the punishment is directly related to the rules that have been violated.

I believe that children should *not* be paid for individual chores around the house. In my opinion, it's as inappropriate for a child to be paid for specific chores as it would be for parents to be paid by their children at the end of each meal. A child who is paid for completing individual tasks will not develop a feeling that her efforts are an integral part of the overall cooperative effort needed to keep the family going.

While parents cannot absolutely dictate what their children should do with their money, they should certainly offer opinions or reactions to what children buy—as long as what they say is constructive and not deprecatory. Ridiculing a child, or telling her that she's stupid doesn't do any good. Explaining to her that what she has bought is a poor value for her money, and telling her why, would be far more useful. While it's necessary to emphasize the importance of money, it is equally necessary not to place so much value on it that a child feels she has to hoard it.

Some children seem unwilling to spend any of their money. One mother told me that her twelve-year-old son kept track of every penny and even charged other children interest on money he loaned them. This was extreme behavior. Although it may seem far-fetched, this sort of miserly attitude toward money can have its beginning in toilet training. When toilet training is coercive and the parent places great value on the child's bowel movements, the child sometimes holds back and "hoards" her feces. She is trying to keep to herself something to which her parents give enormous value. If a parent's greatest approval comes only when the child does the right amount in the right place at the right time, her feces have become "currency" for interacting with her parents, and can be used to exert power over her parents by how she controls her bowel movements. I recommend a relaxed and matter-of-fact attitude about toilet training to help avoid such behavior patterns. If your child hoards her allowance to an extreme degree, encourage her to be more flexible and let her know that she should use some of her money for her own pleasure and perhaps share these pleasures with her friends. Let her know that charging interest on loans to her friends is hardly a friendly gesture and can cause her to be looked upon as strange, or perhaps even to be rejected by them.

ANGER
(SEE ALSO *Aggression, Arguments Between Parents, Child Abuse, Crying, Head Banging, Infancy, Love-Hate Relationships, Sibling, Temper Tantrums, Withdrawn Child*)

There are any number of sources of frustration and anger in a child's life. For an infant, frustration comes when her needs are not fulfilled—if she cries and no one comes, for instance. For an older child, the feeling that she is not faring well in school or with friends or siblings may cause her to become frustrated or angry. Or she may simply be angry at her parents if they don't give her what she wants. Whatever the cause, anger is an inevitable part of life, and parents need to help their child deal with it in a constructive way.

You should bear in mind that your child learns how to deal with emotions by observing her parents. If parents are prone to angry outbursts, the child is likely to imitate this behavior. If parents avoid expressing anger directly, but become tight-lipped and white-faced instead, or sulk silently, the child will imitate this sort of response.

None of the patterns described above is a positive, constructive way of dealing with anger. The best way to deal with anger is to express it in words—without demeaning other people's character. The best place to do this, in my opinion, is in the home, in the security of a loving relationship between parents and child. Violent outbursts, on the other hand, can only make things worse and can cause a child to feel unprotected. "If my parents lose control, how can they help me when I'm out of control?'' Unexpressed anger can come out later in such physical symptoms as stomachaches and headaches.

If parents deal with their own feelings of frustration and anger by expressing them verbally, and then attempting to solve the underlying difficulties, they will offer a positive, constructive problem-solving model for their child.

ANOREXIA NERVOSA
(SEE ALSO *Appetite, Food*)

Our culture's emphasis on slenderness and beauty encourages a peculiar disease called anorexia nervosa, an obsession with being thin. Anorexia usually occurs in teenage girls; it is rare in boys. It is estimated that tens of thousands of young women are anorexics. The major symptoms include an intense fear of becoming obese and a weight loss of 25 percent or more. Together with this, there is usually the absence of menstruation, slowed pulse, low blood pressure and body temperature, hyperactivity, and sometimes the growth of fine hair all over the body. Anorexics typically consume only a few hundred calories a day; many also use diuretics, laxatives, and exercise in an effort to become thinner and thinner. In a variation known as bulimarexia, some anorexics consume huge quantities of food and then force themselves to throw it up. Some may spend many hours a week vomiting.

Most anorexics are the kind of dependable, conscientious children who have been so little trouble to their parents that they are often overlooked. The families of anorexics tend to be overprotective and rigid, and to avoid resolving conflicts. The underlying reason for anorexia is a fear of growing up and becoming independent, and particularly a fear of growing up and becoming a woman, having babies, and becoming a mother. There is usually a fear of sexual relationships as well. By their stringent dieting, anorexics achieve a sense of self-mastery. "My eating is the one thing I can control," anorexics typically say. At the same time, they become the focus of family attention and delay entry into adulthood. Without proper treatment, up to 20 percent of the victims of anorexia die from the irreversible effects of chronic starvation. Others are saved by being hospitalized against their wills and force-fed. If you believe that your child shows signs of anorexia, psychological assistance is essential.

APOLOGIZING

Some parents are reluctant to apologize to their children when they knowingly make a mistake or have done something they regret. They fear that they will show weakness to their children, who will then lose respect for them. This is totally incorrect. In fact, the opposite is true. If children are old enough to talk, they are old enough to begin to understand and appreciate their parents saying, "I'm sorry. I made a mistake." Children see their parents as more human, more compassionate, and respect them more for apologizing. More often than not, a child's response will be, "That's okay, Mom. I understand." Not only is it appropriate for a parent to apologize to a child when a mistake is made, but it serves as a model to the child for learning how to apologize to others. It's unfair for a parent to insist that a child apologize when that parent never admits to a mistake.

Forcing a child to apologize when a child feels that no "injustice" was perpetrated may cause a child to feel resentment and anger. Make sure that your insistence that a child apologize to someone else be backed by a concrete misdeed that bears some feeling on the part of the child. For example, I once observed a mother walking down the street with her child. The mother insisted that the child apologize to an adult for bumping into him. It was clearly the adult's clumsiness, and not the child's, that caused the accident. However, the mother felt that the child should apologize since the other person involved was an adult. In my opinion, this parent should not have insisted that her child apologize.

Sometimes an apology can be a double-edged sword: Some children have learned to apologize constantly as a means of avoiding responsibility. In fact, they apologize so well that they refuse compliments and encouragement. I've also known children who feel that all they have to do is apologize and they've undone any misdeed. I think in particular of one child who misbehaved toward another child, apologized, and whose mother then received this compliment from the mistreated child's father: "Your son apologizes so beautifully." The mother replied, "He should. He's had a lot of practice!" If you notice that your child fits into this category, and frivolously repeats impoliteness, disrespect, or tardiness, followed by an apology, make it clear that an apology is not meant to be an excuse for knowingly doing "wrong" things.

APPETITE
(SEE ALSO *Anorexia Nervosa, Food, Obesity*)

From infancy, most children will go through periods when their eating habits vary enormously. Babies, for instance, may spit out food because of their growing sense of independence and the need to assert themselves. As long as your pediatrician is satisfied that your child is healthy and developing normally, I don't think you should be overly concerned. You can gradually increase your child's curiosity about tasting by offering her "finger foods"—bits of fruit, cereal, small pieces of meat, or other small morsels that she can pick up and put in her mouth. Also, if you give her more of the things that she likes and less of the things she spits out, your baby is apt to eat more.

In my experience I have often seen older children who eat little at mealtime, something that is an affront to some adults. Generations of children have been admonished with "There are starving children in the world!" I think this can make meals unpleasant and take the joy out of eating with others. I don't think you can insist that a child eat everything you serve, although I do think it is fair to expect that a child at least taste new foods, without necessarily finishing whole portions.

Some finickiness about food is natural with older children, and it does not necessarily indicate that they will be poor eaters the rest of their lives. However, when parents over-react to a child's eating habits, the youngster may engage in a power struggle in an attempt to control adults. While hunger isn't a satisfying feeling, controlling or "getting even" with insistent adults can be a child's motivation in refusing to eat. When parents express great concern over a child's eating, the child may rebel by an apparent lack of interest in food.

I think a more relaxed approach is more conducive to healthy development and getting a picky eater to eat. Offer food casually and without pushing. Let children take their time eating; it's not unusual for young children to play a bit with their food. If your child steadfastly refuses to eat, you might simply say, "Well, I guess you're not hungry," and take the plate away.

From a practical point of view, it is impossible for a parent to prevent a child from eating "junk" food from time to time. Even if you don't have high-calorie, low-nutrition foods in your home, children spend time with other children who do have access to them. While I am not a specialist in nutrition, my personal view is that you should do whatever possible to limit your child's intake of "junk" food, without being harsh about it. The first step is to keep non-nutritious food out of the house. Experience tells me that children can enjoy fresh fruit and raw vegetables as snacks just as much as "junk" food. Let your children know that good nutrition, which can help them avoid illness, is something you value, and eventually they will adopt your attitude. I also think it is important for you to make certain that breakfast and dinner, the meals your children are most likely to eat at home, be balanced nutritionally in order to compensate for the "junk" food they may be eating outside the home.

ARGUMENTS BETWEEN PARENTS
(SEE ALSO *Aggression, Anger, Custody, Divorce, Love-Hate Relationships, Temper Tantrums*)

Children are taught to deal with life's problems by the experiences they have as they grow up, and the lessons they learn from those who love and protect them are usually the most impressive. In the course of life, children will be bound to see arguments arise among those close to them. Arguments in a sense represent an attempt to resolve differences of opinion in a verbal way. The best way for children to learn how to resolve differences of opinion verbally is to see that their parents can argue heatedly and still love each other. Of course, I am not talking about violent battles, or name-calling. It is frightening for children to see that the people on whom they rely for protection are out of control.

Parents who attempt to hide their disagreements from their children by arguing only behind closed doors are losing the opportunity to teach their children that it's okay to be angry at times, even with those they love; that anger does not mean the annihilation of the person with whom they are angry; and that people can express their feelings and resolve their conflicts with words. Moreover, parents who attempt to hide their disagreements from their children will usually not meet with much success. Children are very sensitive to feelings, and are only too aware when their parents are angry or upset with each other.

If children are never exposed to their parents' arguments, they may feel guilty when they themselves become annoyed or angry with someone they love. In my work with adult patients, I have frequently found that those who could not handle their anger and were frightened of their negative feelings had come from homes where they had never seen or heard their parents argue. In a sense, they never learned how to deal with their own feelings of ambivalence, anger, or hostility. In their relationships with members of the opposite sex, these people were terrified of emotional involvement, simply because they sensed that there was no way they could fall in love with somebody and not have momentary feelings of anger toward that person. When these people felt angry, their response was to immediately leave the relationship. I believe that it is important for parents to help children learn how to deal with negative feelings, and how to resolve conflicts with those they love in a way that will lead to a constructive relationship. Instead of hiding their disagreements from their children, parents can acknowledge that there may indeed be strong differences of opinion. They can then do their best to resolve their differences of opinion verbally.

ASTHMA

Asthma is a chronic allergic condition that is the result of a narrowing of the bronchial tubes due to spasm, swelling, mucous, or a combination of these. The asthmatic feels as if he is choking and may wheeze as he struggles to get sufficient air. Asthma is the leading chronic illness in children. However, parents will be heartened to know that most children outgrow asthma. Even if the attacks don't disappear completely, they do become less severe.

What makes a child asthmatic? Allergists tend to consider asthma the result of sensitivity to environmental elements, such as animal hair, dust, mold, or pollen. Many psychotherapists believe that emotional conflicts either cause asthma or trigger it. Some maintain that thinking of all asthma as caused by a single factor may not be realistic; that there are different kinds of asthma, such as the infective type, which results from a bacteria or virus; the allergic type; the psychological type; and other types that represent combinations of causes. In my opinion, asthma has a physical cause. In a study I conducted, I found that asthmatics experienced more difficulties around the time of birth. However, I also believe that tension and stress can precipitate an asthma attack. I have treated some children who find that asthmatic symptoms cause their parents to pay more attention to them. These children may unconsciously take advantage of this situation when they feel threatened, angry, or unloved. This, of course, creates a paradox for the parents, who want to help their child but at the same time do not want to encourage asthmatic symptoms as an attention-getting mechanism.

You can help your child avoid asthmatic reactions by helping him avoid the elements that trigger his attacks. If the attacks are related to household dust, frequent wet-mopping and dusting (when the child is not in the room) will help; if you notice a link between tension and asthma attacks, you can help your child avoid stress. I recommend that you take your child to an allergist, who can test your youngster for allergies and prescribe treatment.

ATTENTION-GETTING
(SEE ALSO *Bragging, Cheating, Crying, Juvenile Delinquency, Lying, Sibling, Stealing, Whining*)

Young children often seek attention for new accomplishments: "Watch me button my shirt," "See how I can do this puzzle." They are looking for approval out of pride in their newly mastered task. Adolescents often show off to gain the admiration of the opposite sex. However, children who are constantly showing off, whining, or doing something shocking or destructive to gain attention are troubled. If your child is always trying to be the center of attention, you should try to examine why he should feel the need for this extra notice. Often, such a child desperately wants his parents' approval and should not be punished for "acting up." He is trying to tell you that he feels neglected, and is probably insecure as a result. As a rule, children whose parents pay attention to them early in life will not feel the need to be the center of attention all the time.

There is an exception to this rule, however. Some parents, by focusing all their attention on their child, and attempting to focus everyone else's attention on him, can easily set in motion a pattern that could lead to the child's exhibitionistic behavior. This is not only a disservice to the child; it is a problem for everyone else who comes in contact with that family. I am thinking in particular of a gathering of family and friends that an acquaintance described to me. A couple brought their four-year-old son into a roomful of adults who were engaged in conversation. The couple proceeded to place their child in the middle of the room, surround him with books, coloring books, crayons, and puzzles—as if the room were a nursery school. The mother announced that "Brian wants to make a picture for everyone." Of course, out of politeness all the adults interrupted their conversations and focused on Brian's artistic efforts. At dinner, Brian's mother announced that, "Brian loves broccoli." Everyone watched Brian eat broccoli—with his fingers, scattering pieces on the table, the floor, and his lap. When Brian's mother informed everyone that "Brian wants *more* broccoli," it seemed as if the group were expected to burst into applause. When, at last, mother, father, and Brian left, there was a sigh of relief from the other guests. This family needed—and eventually did seek—help. They over-valued their child, made him the constant focus of their attention, and expected everyone else to do the same. With therapy, the parents were able to stop this destructive pattern.

AUTISM
(SEE ALSO *Schizophrenia*)

Autism, or infantile autism, which is also referred to as childhood schizophrenia, is a rare mental disease that affects about .03% of the population at any given time. Autism generally appears in the first year of life. The autistic child may rock back and forth, or bang his head repeatedly; he may stare into space for long periods of time; he doesn't make eye-to-eye contact with people, and is unable to communicate normally. Some parents describe the autistic child as a "good" baby, because he makes no demands at all on the parents during that first year of life. In fact, the autistic baby frequently doesn't even indicate that he is hungry. The autistic child does not respond to affection. When he's picked up, he may arch his back and pull away.

Later, the autistic child may learn to speak and then after learning may stop speaking; sometimes the autistic child, although of normal intelligence, may not be able to speak until he is four or five years old. The autistic child may be unable to distinguish between animate and inanimate objects, and sometimes becomes preoccupied with household appliances. One child I treated was so preoccupied with toilets that he spent hours at a time flushing the toilet, and had to immediately examine the toilets wherever he went. Another child I treated showed a similar preoccupation with stoves. He would draw them, examine them, open and shut doors.

Some professionals regard autism as basically a communication disorder. In my opinion, autism has a neurological or physical basis, and is sometimes precipitated by environmental conditions. I believe that autism may have its basis in an inborn defect in the child's neurological development time-table. I have sometimes felt that a child who is physically predisposed to autism can be prevented from developing it by a great deal of parental cuddling, holding, and stimulation. However, because babies who are predisposed to autism make so few demands on their parents, parents may indeed fail to provide them with just the stimulation they need. Autism is extremely resistant to treatment. Progress has been made in treating autistic children, but it requires enormous inputs of time, energy, and emotion.

Because we see autistic *behavior* in children who have been severely deprived of stimulation in their first year of life, I believe that some children who are diagnosed as autistic have become that way due to a lack of parental care, love, and responsiveness. For this reason, I encourage all parents to pick up, hold, cuddle, talk to, and stimulate their babies often. Even if the baby seems to show little interest in parental involvement in the first year of life, I strongly believe that parents should offer it anyway. Many parents are afraid to do this for fear that they will "spoil" the baby. This will never spoil a child, and it may serve to prevent the development of autistic behavior.

B

BABYSITTER
(SEE ALSO *Day Care, Separation Anxiety, Sleep, Television*)

I think it is a good idea to begin to use occasional babysitters soon after you come home from the hospital. They will give you a chance to get away from your baby now and then to tend to other matters, and they will also get your baby used to being handled by others from time to time. At first you may find it difficult to leave anyone else in charge of your child. This is a perfectly normal and natural feeling. In fact, some people choose never to have babysitters. They take their children with them everywhere. While I have no theoretical objection to this approach, if you are forced to be away from your child later on for one reason or another, your child will have a difficult time suddenly adjusting to another person's caring for him.

Almost anyone can take care of your baby's physical needs. His emotional needs are the ones with which I am most concerned, since these have the greatest effect on his growing personality. Needless to say, the people you choose as babysitters for your infant or young child should be warm, understanding, well adjusted, and above all, they should enjoy children. It is far easier to list these qualities, however, than to define them. Watch out for people who are overly concerned with neatness and cleanliness, since they generally put those interests before the emotional needs of your child. People who are inclined to dominate you would probably undermine the relationship between you and your child. People who are depressed or have some personality characteristic that keeps them from being lighthearted and spontaneous might be unable to give your growing child the kind of stimulation he needs.

I would be cautious about leaving a child in the care of a sibling. If an accident occurred in your absence and the smaller child were hurt, it would be a tremendous burden of guilt for the older child to bear.

I think it is most helpful to rely on your instincts in choosing someone to care for your child in your absence. You can usually almost "feel" whether a given person will be able to care for your child in a way that makes the child feel secure and comfortable. The most crucial point to consider is how your child feels about that person. Children generally like people who enjoy them and dislike those who don't. No matter how qualified the person may be, if your child is fearful or anxious, or if you feel somewhat apprehensive about the person's sensitivity to your child, respect this feeling and act upon it.

Remember that children often establish their attitudes about people by using their parents' responses as guides. If it becomes apparent that the babysitter is a friendly person acceptable to you, your child will most likely accept the babysitter too. If you do not feel comfortable with a particular babysitter, do not hesitate to send that person away. You must—absolutely must—feel comfortable with the babysitter who is caring for your child.

Be sure there is enough time to let your baby become familiar with the babysitter before you leave. Generally speaking, this takes between a half an hour and an hour. The exact amount of time varies with the age and temperament of your child and also with his familiarity with the babysitter. While this may seem like a tedious process to go through, it will have long-range benefits and will serve to help your child master any fears he may have of strangers.

Even though newborn babies apparently show little awareness of strangers, it is still important to have the babysitter come early so that there is no chance that your baby will be apprehensive. Incidentally, you should also arrange for the sitter to come while your child is awake. I cannot tell you how many times I have seen sleep disturbances develop because a baby wakes up to find a stranger caring for him after he was put down to sleep by his parents. Under no circumstances should you sneak away when you are going out. It is far better for your child to be aware of your leaving, even if he cries, than it is for you to hide your going to prevent him from crying. You will only create far more stress that just might have very bad long-term effects.

Having a steady parade of different babysitters, none of whom is particularly familiar to your child, can cause your child to become apprehensive about strangers. He begins to associate a stranger with a separation from his parents. Since he doesn't like the separation, he doesn't like the stranger. And making frequent changes can have more serious effects. In my professional practice, I frequently encounter serious emotional problems in children who have had lots of different people caring for them. The child is thus prevented from ever having a continuing relationship with adults.

It usually works best to have perhaps two or three babysitters that you call upon occasionally. But make sure that all of them are responsive to your child's emotional needs in a way that is consistent with your philosophy of childrearing.

BABY TALK
(SEE ALSO *Language Development Problems*)

Many adults insist on talking "baby talk" even as their children grow older. This tends to keep the children infantile and reflects the adult's need more than the child's. Some people enjoy keeping their child dependent and babylike, even when the child is capable of and struggling for more independence. Children generally resent being talked down to in this way, and they are far more trusting and respectful of people who speak to them in a forthright manner that does not demean them.

While infantile words themselves won't ultimately harm a child's language development, they can affect his self-image and social relationships. A child who attends nursery school, for example, and has a vocabulary filled with "cutesy" words may be teased by other children or perhaps regarded as immature by his teachers. Also, if a youngster visits a friend's house and politely asks for "nummies" (instead of food), confusion is likely to result and the child's attempts at meaningful communication will be impeded.

31

If your child picks up baby talk from someone outside your household you should discourage his infantile speech by making it clear that you do not care to communicate when he speaks in this way. Ask him to speak more clearly and more properly before you respond. In this way, you will demonstrate that your child will not be rewarded for infantile behavior or speech.

BASHFULNESS
(SEE ALSO *Withdrawn Child*)

Bashfulness in children is not unusual. Many children feel shy at one time or another. If your child is *always* in his own world, however, and seems unable to ever interact socially, this may reflect an emotional problem that requires professional help. A key question is whether your child is able, even in his fantasies, to maintain a sense of reality. I remember that my own son, Eric, played by himself a great deal at age three and a half. Once his nursery school teacher saw him staring at a toy car that he had parked in a toy garage. Eric sat motionless for such a long time that the teacher finally asked, "Eric, wouldn't you like to play with the other children?" He said, "No, I can't. This car is broken and in the garage —I'm waiting for the garage man to fix it." His teacher was concerned about Eric's absorption in fantasy, but I was convinced that this was not a problem because even in his fantasy he had a healthy grip on reality: he knew that it takes a long time to have a car fixed. By the way, the next year a different teacher was worried about Eric. She said he always played with other children—rarely by himself! Many parents often get such reactions from their children's teachers. There is just no hard-and-fast rule about the "normal" amount of time a child should spend alone or with others.

BATHING

For a young child, a bath can be as frightening as it can be pleasurable. Many young children have been accidentally doused in a tub or inadvertently frightened when stinging soap got in their eyes. It might take just a few such incidents to convince a child that water is scary and something to be avoided. Once children become frightened in this way, it takes a great deal of patience to help them overcome it. I think it is important to try to help a child overcome these fears as quickly as possible, especially when such a reaction appears during infancy or early childhood. If you indicate your understanding of your child's anxieties and fears, you can help her relax and think of bath time as "fun."

Children between two and four years of age sometimes get very anxious when the water is drained while they are still in the tub. They fear that they will be sucked down the drain with the water. Even if you try to show them that they are too big to be pulled down the drain, their anxiety remains. This occurs because children this age sometimes feel they can magically "grow small" in an instant, like Alice in Wonderland. Some television cartoons reinforce this feature by showing creatures who do get pulled through small openings as a result of becoming small. A young child sees this as real, and not a technological trick. If your child shows this fear, simply wait until he is out of the tub before you open the drain.

BEDWETTING
(SEE ALSO *Regression, Soiling, Toilet Training*)

Sometimes bedwetting (also called enuresis) is a result of a constitutional or hereditary inability to wake up when the bladder is full. This occurs more frequently in males than females. Thus, in some families bedwetting occurs well into childhood and then seems to subside spontaneously in early adolescence. Most of the time, a child's loss of bladder control is related to emotional tension. He may be feeling pressured by the arrival of a new sibling, starting school, his parents' divorce, or moving to a new place. In such cases, parental support, reassurance, and reduction of stress will serve to eliminate this symptom. If the problem persists, an evaluation should be made by your pediatrician and perhaps a neurologist and also a psychologist.

Children who have been bowel-trained very early (before two years of age) may have trouble controlling their bladders even if they can control their bowels.

In most cases, I think bedwetting is due to some organic factor. Parents should consult a pediatrician so that he or she can check for physical causes. Some doctors prescribe medication that helps children avoid wetting at night. Others may recommend electronic devices that wake children up as soon as they are wet, but I am opposed to these. I have treated sexually impotent adult male patients whose problems seemed in some way related to such conditioning when they were children. These devices do work, but not without some psychological risk. I believe it is more important for children to learn to use their own resources to achieve control.

I do recommend, however, that you get an alarm clock that rings loudly and place it some distance from your child's bed. Have him set it himself to ring three or four hours after he goes to sleep. After getting out of bed to turn off the alarm, he can make a trip to the bathroom, and then reset the clock for three or four hours later. Gradually the alarm can be set for a longer and longer time interval. This will eventually help him overcome his problem.

This method enables him to use his own resources for overcoming his problem. Under no circumstances should you shame or humiliate a child who wets the bed.

Some children wet the bed as an expression of anger toward a parent, which they are fearful of doing directly. By allowing his bedwetting to be a great inconvenience to you, you are reinforcing this as a pattern of behavior for expression of his anger. I therefore recommend that the child change his own sheets if he is old enough, and if not, that he assist you in doing it.

BEHAVIOR MODIFICATION
(SEE ALSO *Allowance, Discipline and Punishment, Responsibility, Rewards, Toilet Training*)

Behavior modification, or behavior therapy, attempts to alleviate problems by applying scientific principles derived mainly from experimental psychology. This type of therapy assumes that virtually all human behavior is learned, and that the best way to correct behavior problems is through retraining. Behavior therapy tries to make changes in specific things a person does, rather than in his thoughts or feelings. It emphasizes the here and now, rather than early life events that led up to or caused the present situation. In a way, behavior therapy asks "how" the behavior can be changed. Psychotherapy asks "why" the behavior is present in the first place before it asks how it can be changed. In other words, to the behavior therapist, the behavior itself is the problem. To the psychotherapist, in contrast, the behavior is more likely only an expression or symptom of a more basic emotional disturbance.

I believe strongly that behavior therapy may provide short-term gains, but can possibly lead to long-term losses. I believe that when behavior therapy changes a child's behavior, it may actually be a disservice, since the child's more basic maladjustment remains, and removing the symptom may postpone the child's getting the help necessary to make more fundamental changes in his personality.

Frequently the psychotherapist's objection to behavior therapy is illustrated by comparing emotional illness to physical illness, like appendicitis. The symptoms of appendicitis are soreness of the abdomen, headache, nausea, and fever. Now, aspirin will usually suppress most of these symptoms. But aspirin is certainly no cure for appendicitis! In fact, if aspirin removes the symptoms, the inflammation of the appendix will probably go untreated and will eventually kill the patient.

Likewise, I would advise against even so simple a form of behavior modification as paying a child money for doing specific chores around the house. This behavior modification will probably "work" in the sense that the child will probably do the chores to get the money. However, what is vital here is that if the child is paid for the chores he will never develop the feeling that he is an essential part of the family and his help is part of an overall cooperative effort to keep the whole family going. He may turn out to have little interest in accomplishing much in life unless he is given a material reward. To me, it's as inappropriate for a child to be paid for specific chores as it would be for parents to be paid by their children at the end of each meal.

If parents do wish to investigate the use of behavior therapy in an attempt to change their child's behavior, I strongly advise against their using such techniques themselves, or entrusting them to other family members or even to teachers. I recommend instead that they consult a licensed, certified, experienced behavior therapist.

BOREDOM
(SEE ALSO *Crying, Curiosity, Depression, Gifted Child, Infant, Masturbation, Play, School, Teacher*)

Boredom is one of the most unpleasant human feelings. Most adults are capable of relieving boredom by turning to some activity that provides stimulation or interest. Boredom on the job can lead to frustration, anger, destructiveness, and loss of motivation to perform. Repetitive activities such as assembly line work have been shown to cause workers, on occasion, to deliberately smash an object or put a dent in it. Their purpose was to vent their frustration and break the boring routine. Some of these workers said they simply wanted to do something unique, "to leave my mark."

In much the same way, when a child is bored in school because the work is too simple, or he has an uninspiring teacher, he can lose motivation, daydream, become frustrated and destructive, or neglect his work and become an underachiever. I've seen this pattern very often in intellectually gifted children who are in regular classes. When they are placed in a more stimulating environment, they "blossom" into happier people and their negative behavior subsides.

All children need stimulation. Toddlers are curious and tend to explore, examine, and take things apart and put them together again. The pleasure that comes with the opportunity to explore by having things around to play with and people who facilitate such play, increases the child's motivation to learn and makes for a happier and more interesting child—though a more demanding one. Children whose boredom is a way of life because of the lack of objects to play with or because of severe restrictions or limited contact with stimulating adults frequently turn to whining, tuning out the world by going off to sleep, or sometimes engaging in excessive masturbation to provide some pleasure and stimulation in an otherwise sterile environment.

Babies, too, get bored. Boredom is one of the main reasons a baby cries. Unfortunately, a baby can do little to provide stimulation, since it is helpless. The cry of distress or boredom means, "Pick me up—hold me—cuddle me—show me things—make the environment change." This is frequently the reason a baby stops crying when he is picked up. Don't feel you are spoiling your baby if this happens. I know many parents are told that if you pick up a baby and he stops crying, you will be encouraging him to control you by crying. That just is not so. When the boredom stops, the baby is happy and stops crying. It's not a challenge to you from your baby, but is the only way he can relieve boredom. If you let the baby cry and cry, he will eventually go off to sleep. When this occurs repeatedly, the child learns to go off to sleep as a means of relieving tension and stress. He learns, through this helplessness and the lack of responsiveness of others, that it is hopeless to try, and he gives up easily. Eventually this baby gives up trying altogether. This is a pattern that we call "learned helplessness," and it persists into childhood and even into adult life. Studies have shown that depression in adult life is related to this kind of early parent-child relationship.

By providing stimulation for your child—by picking him up, holding him, cuddling him, talking to him, singing to him, smiling at him, playing with him—you will help him feel that the world does indeed respond to him, that he is important, that he is cared about, that he makes a difference in the world. This will prevent the development of the sense of helplessness that can turn into depression later on.

BOSSINESS
(SEE ALSO *Adolescence, Bully, Defiance*)

Children who become very bossy are sometimes experimenting. They are testing a variety of social approaches. In doing so, they learn about themselves, as well as about the boundaries of acceptable social behavior. Generally, bossiness, in the sense of negativistic or defiant behavior, occurs when a child is around two years of age, again around the ages of seven and eight, and then again during adolescence.

If your child bosses her friends, sooner or later she will run into children who won't tolerate it and who will turn to others for support and companionship. However, it may take some time for your child to realize this. Meanwhile, your job as a parent is to let her know that other children will stop playing with her—and parents will keep their children away from her—if she continues to behave this way. I don't suggest that you be overly critical of her behavior. Simply let her know the consequences of her actions, and at the same time point out ways in which she can enjoy herself without taking such a domineering attitude. Don't hesitate to ask her to apply the golden rule: "How would you like it if other children treated you this way?"

If your child is being bossy with you, her parents, she may be trying to assert her independence, which is quite natural. But it is up to you to channel her behavior into something more socially acceptable. You can do this by asking her advice about things and inviting her to express her feelings, rather than constantly *telling* her what to do. Focus on the positive, and you should find that her argumentative attitude will diminish.

Often children reflect some of their parents' behavior, so it might be helpful for you and your spouse to examine your own actions to see if your child is in fact imitating or identifying with your way of dealing with things. If you yourselves are imperious instead of understanding, or inclined to bicker over small issues, you may find that an alteration in your behavior will lead to an alteration in hers.

BRAGGING
(SEE ALSO *Attention-Getting, Conceit*)

I once worked with a little boy who was clearly neglected by his parents. His father had abandoned him, and his mother, who was a prostitute, paid him scant attention. However, when the boy talked about his mother he said, "My mother makes a barrel of oatmeal cookies every week. A barrel! She always tells me and all my friends, 'Take more, take more, take all you want.' " The facts were quite different. This mother never made cookies for her son, nor did she spend time with him. The child had created a fantasy mother to help him deal with his feelings of rejection and despair.

More frequently, children brag or exaggerate in order to fascinate their friends and gain a sense of importance in the eyes of their peers. It is very common for children to exaggerate details of their lives, even to the point of constructing "facts" that are a mixture of lies and fantasy. When I was a child my friends and I exchanged a series of ever-escalating lies: "My father is stronger than your father." "No, he's not. My father is stronger than yours." "He is not. My father can beat up your father." Today, too, a child might claim that his uncle was a superhero or his father played professional football. Some children may even come to believe what they have conjured up in their own minds.

If your child brags or exaggerates excessively, let him know that people may lose trust in him. Let him know that it's not necessary to do this to get people to accept him. Let him know you're more proud of him when he tells stories accurately than when he brags or exaggerates.

Often children believe their boasting friends who make exaggerated claims. If your child insists that such information is factual, you might explain that it is very natural and admirably loyal to take a friend at his word, but that the friend happens to be making up stories to impress others. Even a grade school child can understand that children sometimes feel a little weak inside and that they tell such stories to make themselves seem more important. Your reaction will help give your child some understanding of his friend's motivation and at the same time should protect him from feeling foolish about believing these "facts." This insight could even stop his own bragging.

BREASTFEEDING
(SEE ALSO *Alcoholism, Obesity, Pacifier, Smoking, Sucking, Weaning*)

I recommend breastfeeding, although I do not take a hard and fast position on the matter. I have seldom encountered a mother who chose to breastfeed and later regretted it. On the other hand, I have spoken with many mothers who regretted having made the decision to bottlefeed.

The milk provided by a human mother is specifically geared to her baby's nutritional needs. Generally, babies develop allergies less frequently to their own mother's milk than to formula. Breastfed babies do not have a sour smell when they spit up their milk, but bottlefed babies do. One other built-in advantage to breastfeeding: through the mother's milk the baby receives antibodies to many diseases, which provide a natural immunity to these diseases in early life. Also, by breastfeeding a mother comes naturally in close physical contact with her baby, which is very important in nurturing the baby emotionally as well.

Whether you are planning to breast- or bottlefeed, you should understand a few things about your baby's emotional needs as they exist right after birth. First, a baby is born with a sucking reflex, and a strong need for sucking satisfaction. This must be gratified if he is to be a happy, satisfied infant and a stable adult. Studies have shown that frustration of this infantile need can lead to adult behavior patterns such as excessive smoking, drinking, or eating, which are attempts to find gratification for these early, frustrated needs.

Strange as it may seem, a newborn baby has no real concept of eating. When his stomach is empty and needs food, the baby will get hunger pangs, which are actually minor stomach contractions. Because these contractions will be moderately uncomfortable, they will generally cause a baby to fret or cry. When this occurs, any baby's need to suck increases because sucking is a baby's primitive way of coping with discomfort. When a mother begins to feed the baby, the sucking need begins to be satisfied. At first, the gratification that a baby obtains while feeding is primarily associated with satisfying his sucking needs. The amount of food consumed is secondary. Breastfeeding, as nature's way, is an excellent system for simultaneously satisfying both the sucking need and the need for food. Breastfed babies get most of their milk in the first few minutes of sucking. This assures that the baby gets the proper amount of nutrient even before the sucking need is completely satisfied. Then the baby continues sucking on the breast not because the baby is hungry but to obtain sufficient sucking satisfaction so he can relax and go to sleep. When the sucking need is satisfied, the baby releases from the mother's breast, relaxes, and generally goes off to a pleasant, relaxing sleep.

Contrast this efficient system with the bottle-fed baby, who gets his milk supply at the same rate during the entire feeding. Parents who bottle feed their infants sometimes find that the baby seems to have an enormous appetite. After consuming one bottle, the infant devours a second and may still want more. In my opinion, it is highly unlikely that the baby actually needs that much food. It is more likely that he may have to consume that amount of food to satisfy his sucking needs completely. If this occurs, I suggest that you get some nipples with small holes so that your baby has to suck a little harder to get his food. In this way, he can gratify his sucking needs completely without consuming an inordinate amount of milk.

In addition to the sucking need, a newborn baby has a distinct need for parental contact. Your baby requires fondling, stroking, warmth, touching, and the sound of your voice as well as the sight of your face. Happily, your baby's need to eat forces the close physical contact that is essential for healthy emotional development. Because of this need, if you decide to bottlefeed, I particularly urge you to hold your baby during feedings.

I am inclined to recommend giving a baby an occasional bottle even if the mother decides to breastfeed, partly to accustom the child to this form of feeding if his mother's absence makes it necessary and partly to give the father an opportunity to feed his baby. In the beginning of such "conditioning" the mother should give the occasional bottle until the baby becomes used to it. If the infant associates breastfeeding with his mother and bottle feeding with others, he may well begin to associate a bottle with separation from his mother.

When should you stop breastfeeding? While some supporters of breastfeeding encourage parents to continue for as long as three years, I am inclined to think that beyond two years, breastfeeding tends to increase a baby's dependency on his mother. Whenever you decide to stop breastfeeding, don't force your baby to give up the satisfaction that accompanies his sucking. If your baby still needs sucking gratification after you wean him from the breast, use a bottle until his sucking need has been outgrown.

If, after considering this discussion, you are still undecided about whether to breastfeed or bottlefeed, bear this in mind: you shouldn't force yourself to try it if you feel strongly against it. Breastfeeding works well for most mothers, perhaps because nature intended that it should. But you must enjoy it and so must your baby. Basically, that's really more important to your child's sound psychological development than the source of supply.

BULLY
(SEE ALSO *Bossiness, Bragging, Gang*)

Children rarely bully others unless they have some underlying fear, particularly a feeling of inadequacy. Young bullies are trying to reassure themselves about the feeling of strength that basically they do not have. While I am against physical force and violence, I think that when a child is actually being threatened or coerced and it is impossible to settle the situation with words, then physical self-defense is appropriate—and, I think, morally correct.

Encouraging a child to fight back when he is bullied by other youngsters is not inconsistent with a philosophy of non-violence. Most children can easily understand the difference between being the aggressor, who provokes fights, and defending themselves when another person strikes first. You should explain to your child that if he has done his best to avoid a skirmish, it may finally be necessary for him to defend himself. Let him know that even though you are proud of him for not hitting other children, you would understand if he absolutely *had* to hit to defend himself.

If you know that your child is being bullied regularly by other children, I see nothing wrong with intervening on your child's behalf. It may be necessary to contact the school if the bullying is taking place there, or to contact the other children's parents if it occurs elsewhere. By offering protection for your child, you will not make him a "sissy," but will affirm your role as a loving, caring parent.

42

If you are told that your child is bullying another, you should express your disapproval of this kind of behavior. You can point out that it's very upsetting to a person when someone bullies them and that a reputation as a bully can cause a child to lose friends or prospective friends.

In my experience, the children who are bullies have been bullied themselves by one or both parents. They then take out on other children their misery about being intimidated. If your child is a bully, you would do well to examine your own relationship with your child to find out if you have in fact been intimidating, dictatorial, or threatening. If so, you can modify your own approach, and this in turn should diminish the bullying.

C

CHEATING
(SEE ALSO *Juvenile Delinquency, Lying, Stealing*)

If you discover that your child has cheated—for instance, on a school test—you should discuss this with him in a serious and concerned manner, emphasizing that what he did was wrong. It is important for all people to feel a sense of guilt if they cheat. Unfortunately, some schools and parents place such enormous emphasis on grades that some children cheat almost in self-defense against a system that's brutal. Before parents voice their moral outrage to their child regarding his cheating, they might consider the situation in which their child has been placed. Another element they might consider is whether they themselves cheat on their income taxes, falsify insurance claims, or more or less openly do other things that are wrong, rationalizing that, "Everybody does it," and "It's okay to do it—unless you get caught." It's hard to convince our children that cheating is wrong if we are doing such things, and when numerous elected officials have been convicted of crimes and others have gone free despite clear-cut lying, cheating, and other wrongs.

If your child is found to cheat, I believe you should let your child know that you are deeply concerned about such behavior, but I do not believe that you should be excessively punitive. In all likelihood your child's cheating will be an isolated event. However, if your child's cheating is persistent or chronic, it may be a symptom of an emotional problem. Some children cheat in the hope that they will get caught, which might embarrass their parents and at the same time lead them to provide the attention that the child needs. You may need to seek professional help to find out what is leading your child to such behavior—and, it is hoped, to bring it to an end.

CHILD ABUSE
(SEE ALSO *Anger, Family, Father, Mother*)

Some people assume that parents who abuse their children must hate them. This is not really the case. Usually, people who abuse their children are people who have little control over their impulses; when frustrated, they lash out destructively against those closest to them and least able to defend themselves. Many child abusers were beaten themselves as children. They never learned how to deal with their own anger and aggression.

I've known many young mothers—particularly unwed mothers—who became child abusers because they tried to compensate for the lack of love in their own lives by having a baby they believed would love them and give them the feeling of being important. Then the young mothers discovered that their babies could not fulfill their emotional needs, and that in fact the babies made great demands on them, which they were emotionally incapable of fulfilling. Often, the response was extreme frustration, and sometimes the rage that can lead to child abuse.

But child abuse is by no means restricted to one group of people; nor is it restricted to physical abuse. All kinds of parents, including wealthy and well-educated couples, inflict all kinds of abuse, including emotional abuse and neglect, on their children. Many people are unable or unwilling to accept the real responsibilities of parenthood, and their disappointment and discouragement increases as they encounter the normal problems of everyday life with their children. A father may work seven days a week, insisting that he does so to support his children, but he may hardly have a kind word for them. A mother may spend all day every day with her children and yet may never see them as individuals who have thoughts and feelings of their own. She may instead view them as extensions of herself.

There is no doubt in my mind that something must be done to protect children from the deplorable child abuse going on—the black eyes and broken limbs. Re-educating society about how and why such situations come about is one way of making changes. In addition, people must be willing to get involved if they suspect such abuse. Every state has some facility for dealing with child abuse, and it's possible for people to report suspected cases without giving their own identity. Anyone who suspects that a child is being battered should ask the local telephone operator for a listing of child-protection services in the area; if the telephone operator cannot help, a member of the clergy or a member of the local police department or social service agency should be able to do so. At the same time, I think people must show the same concern about emotional neglect or abuse, which seems less dramatic, but can be even more damaging to children in the long run.

CHILDBIRTH
(SEE ALSO *Family, Father, Mother, Prematurity, Sex Education*)

I think childbirth is a family experience, not a medical experience. It should be a time of shared happiness and excitement. In my view, it is critically important for the integrity of the family to be maintained at the time of childbirth. Fathers should not be relegated to a waiting room, or taken away from their wives. In recent years the medical community has begun to recognize the importance of "bonding," that is, the attachment of parents to their newborn babies. This process is facilitated by close physical contact between parents and child right at the time of birth. When a woman is heavily sedated during delivery she is too weak to hold her baby immediately after birth; she cannot hold or cuddle her baby until after she comes out of the anesthesia. For this reason, I believe we should avoid using sedation and anesthesia unless it's absolutely necessary. Instead, painkillers that do not interfere with the woman's consciousness or control are preferable.

I believe very strongly in childbirth education, and encourage mothers and fathers to share these experiences by taking classes together. It's also important for children in the family to know about the impending birth of the new baby. Children should be encouraged to ask questions, and their questions as to where the baby is growing, how and where it comes out, and all the details of childbirth itself that the children are capable of understanding should be answered. In recent years children have been introduced into the delivery room to observe the birth of a new brother or sister. While this has been controversial, I think it can be a positive experience for children provided that they have been carefully prepared to know what will take place. Books, films, and video cassettes about childbirth can help prepare a child, and during the birth an adult should be available to explain what's happening and to answer any questions. Sharing in the excitement and joy of their mother's giving birth with the closeness and coaching of their father can have an enormous emotional impact on children.

At a United Nations conference a few years ago, I proposed that hospitals provide an intimate and romantic celebration for a new mother and father after the birth of their baby. Having the couple share their first meal as parents with candlelight, wine, and flowers conveys the message that the birth of a baby should be regarded not as a medical phenomenon but as a fulfilling event in the couple's life together, an event to be celebrated with a warm, close, loving toast to their new family.

CLUB
(SEE ALSO *Gang*)

It's quite common for children to form clubs. However, to my mind, the purpose of such clubs is generally to keep people out, rather than to include people. I am reminded of a wonderful book, *The Sneetches,* by Dr. Seuss. In this book only Sneetches who have stars on their bellies can go to a certain beach. Enter a character who knows how to put stars on the bellies of the other Sneetches. Now the Sneetches who first had the stars want theirs removed! I believe that encouraging the kinds of clubs, such as fraternities and sororities, that restrict membership to an "elite," runs counter to the spirit of human understanding. These groups may enhance the self-image of those who belong, but since a larger number of people are excluded, the clubs can make many people unhappy. Restricted clubs can cause the formation of cliques of people who can be narrow in their focus and who can develop a false sense of their importance.

Some schools promote clubs, and children may make every effort to be accepted. As a parent I don't think you should interfere, but I do think you should convey to your children the meaning of these clubs and the feeling of rejection they can cause.

Of course, I don't include Boy Scouts, Girl Scouts, Camp Fire, Boys Clubs of America. Organizations like these have as their focus meeting the needs of children and providing information, stimulation, skills, and social opportunities, as well as community service.

CONCEIT
(SEE ALSO *Attention-Getting, Bragging*)

The conceited child is frequently considered by peers as well as adults to be exhibiting unpleasant, if not obnoxious, behavior. Expressing pride in accomplishments is one thing, but constantly bragging or attempting to draw compliments from people can interfere with relationships. Conceited children frequently belittle other people and any activity that has no meaning to them or in which they do not participate. Such behavior is a mechanism of defense, which is a way of avoiding anxiety. In other words, by demeaning things at which they don't do well, they reduce their anxiety about their own poor performance. In general, conceit reflects underlying feelings of inadequacy, and represents an attempt on the part of the child to compensate for his feelings of weakness by trying to make others think he is stronger, more powerful, or more important than he really is.

Sometimes conceited behavior is learned, and in a sense imitates the parents' own tendency to "highlight" or exaggerate their own achievements. If your child shows conceit, stop and examine your own behavior first. Then you might point out to your child that constant bragging can make people turn against you or want to avoid being with you. Try to present this view in a non-threatening way; we know that children who seem conceited really feel inadequate, so they may be supersensitive to criticism. It would also be a good idea to respond to your child's display of conceit by pointing out that your love and acceptance of that child are absolutely unconditional—they have nothing to do with the child's accomplishments. In this way, you can help your child gain the true confidence and self-esteem that will make bragging, showing off, and conceited behavior unnecessary.

CONSCIENCE
(SEE ALSO *Discipline and Punishment, Guilt*)

A child who establishes a sense of right and wrong is one who has a "conscience." He develops this conscience by internalizing the values of his parents and the discipline with which he was reared. In effect a conscience is the code of ethics that exists within a person. When this code is violated—that is, when the person does something immoral or illegal—the person has feelings of guilt. Since these guilt feelings are unpleasant, the person is motivated to avoid them and thus do the "right" thing.

If a child does not develop an effective conscience, if he lacks an internalized set of values, he is inclined to act on impulse, no matter what damage he may cause to others. Usually, the only thing a "conscienceless" person worries about is being caught and punished. He has no concept of right and wrong; often, his behavior is unacceptable. I strongly believe that consistent discipline is a way to develop civilized behavior and a strong sense of right and wrong —in other words, an ethical sense.

CRYING
(SEE ALSO *Boredom, Infancy, Whining*)

To my mind babies cry for four basic reasons. One, out of boredom: They need stimulation and attention and need to be held, carried, talked to, and fondled. Two, often children cry because they are tired and need to be rocked or given some other help in relaxing so they can fall asleep. Three, many babies cry because of their need for sucking gratification; they generally satisfy this need during feeding and in those extra moments of nursing that take place after they have had their fill of food. Four, babies cry because of physical discomfort, because something is too cold or too hot or poking them, or because of some pain they feel inside. Colic, which I discuss below, is among those physical pains.

In early life, crying is your child's way of signaling his distress, the first "language" with which he can communicate his needs. If you respond to your baby's cry during this early stage, he will come to see the world as a safe and satisfying place. The baby who is left to "cry it out" may develop a sense of isolation and distrust and may turn inward by tuning out the world that will not respond to him. Later on in life, this child may continue to cope with stress by trying to shut out reality.

I am absolutely against letting a baby cry it out, yet this common advice—often given by pediatricians, other professionals, or friends —is actually endorsed by some esteemed child-care experts. They feel that you will spoil the child if you pick him up when he is crying. But I contend that no baby is spoiled by cuddling. Satisfying a baby's infantile need to be held and comforted makes that need go away so that the child can get on with other tasks in his early development.

When constant crying continues, it may seem that nothing you do provides relief. This can make parents tense, nervous, and frustrated, an irritability that is communicated to the child, making matters even worse. If a child is crying incessantly he may be experiencing the harsh pain of colic, which occurs when the baby's formula disagrees with his digestive system and gas pressure builds up. As the digestive system begins to mature, these problems subside. But if your baby seems colicky, discuss this with your pediatrician, who may advise changing the formula.

Even though picking up your crying infant may not seem to help, you should continue to cuddle your baby and offer as much comfort as possible. He still benefits from the closeness and warmth of being held in your arms.

An older child who cries frequently is probably sending similar signals to his parents: "I need you. Please pay attention to me." Children should be encouraged to express their feelings; if they are forced to hold back their tears, they will be encouraged to bottle up their emotions. This could be the start of an emotional pattern that can set off great inner tension in the years ahead and such tension can produce physical illnesses in some cases. However, just being able to express emotions is not enough. You must help your child learn how to cope with the problems that *cause* unpleasant feelings in order for him to gain a sense of mastery over some of life's stresses.

CURIOSITY
(SEE ALSO *Learning, Play*)

From the moment they are born, children are curious about the world around them. Infants a few days old are fascinated by colored mobiles, lights, wallpaper, textures. By the time a baby is three months old he can begin to grasp objects and become even more aware of his environment. Once the child is old enough to crawl and walk, he will need some extra supervision to insure that he doesn't hurt himself. Most parents have "baby-proofed" the house by the time the child starts to move about.

In early childhood some toddlers are livelier than others and tend to explore in a physical way; others explore the world in a more mental way through their fantasies. Parents often ask me how to deal with the child who is constantly taking falls and crashing about the house in a seemingly reckless manner. For the most part, such children are simply exhibiting their curiosity about the world and should be given freedom to do so while at the same time being protected from obvious dangers such as open windows, and staircases. However, constant warnings about every little possible danger will eventually cause the child to either tune you out or become so cautious that he will be too frightened to explore.

Preschool children are likely to badger parents constantly with questions that always seem to start with "how" or "why." It may seem trying at times, but if you attempt to answer your child's questions as best you can, he will grow up knowing he can always come to you for guidance, truthfulness, and loving support.

Being a psychologist doesn't preclude my having to face the normal problems every other parent encounters. Once I was deeply engrossed in editing the material for one of my books, and my daughter, Pia, then around eight years old, periodically thrust question after question at me. After answering the first dozen or so, I finally blurted out, "Can't you please stop asking questions for a while? Don't you see I'm busy?" Her reply was, "If you don't ask questions, how are you ever going to learn?" For this reason, it's important for parents, as busy as you are, to at least show respect for your child's curiosity, and to avoid at all costs putting even a little dent in that wonderful quality.

CUSTODY
(SEE ALSO *Divorce*)

I believe we should change the concept of child "custody" to something more appropriate. For one thing, custody implies ownership, and no parent really owns a child. Philosophically speaking, children belong to the world. When parents bring children into the world they are assuming the commitment and responsibility to provide the optimal conditions for that child's healthy physical and emotional growth. Another reason why "custody" is inappropriate is that it is an abrasive term, particularly as it's used in law courts. People "win" custody or "lose" custody; someone is "awarded" custody, and people "fight" for custody. The term itself can set parents apart with increased anger and hostility. It would be more appropriate to consider *responsibility* as the issue, rather than custody. Clearly, if judges or those in positions to decide on the care of children following divorce directed *responsibility* to either or both parents, it would have a different tone than deciding who "wins" and who "loses" custody. For the time being, however, I will use the legal term of "custody."

In most states, the law stipulates that "the best interest of the child" should be given primary consideration in deciding which parent gets custody after a divorce. Coupled with the "equal access" law, which mandates that both parents have equal rights to custody, the best interest concept is fair. If these laws are interpreted properly, they mean a judge must determine which parent would be better able to meet the physical and emotional needs of the child when deciding who shall have custody.

Historically, the question, "Who will get custody of the children?" was hardly ever asked. Judges often assumed that mothers were innately better equipped than fathers to raise children. I do not believe mothers or fathers should be given custody of a child based on their gender. Happily, courts are beginning to come around to this viewpoint, albeit slowly.

Judges are beginning to look for the following qualities in a parent's attitudes and feelings toward a child: Does the parent consistently express deep love and affection? Is the parent involved in the child's life in a way that nurtures emotional growth? When both parents want custody and each feels equally competent to handle the child's needs, the situation requires very careful evaluation and adjudication.

It is important for parents to seriously examine the question, "Do I *really* want custody of my children?" I know that it is frequently painful to answer that question honestly. Many parents secretly wish they never had children in the first place. This is very hard to admit. Often, after a divorce, parents want time alone to re-evaluate their lives. Having children around may be an extra burden with which they may not want to cope. If a parent sincerely does not want custody of the children, I would advise against seeking it. Your feelings will naturally be reflected in your attitude toward your children. If you are truly concerned with your children's best interests, you will ignore any criticism that you are "abandoning" them. If you feel that your spouse is indeed a better parent, do not hesitate to relinquish custody—provided your spouse and children agree.

If you relinquish custody of your children, this does not mean you are an unfit parent. It is a fact of life that not all people are equally good at all things, and parenthood is no exception. Foremost, you should be concerned with how you really feel about your children; with who is truly the better parent psychologically; and with what your children's wishes are in regard to living arrangements. In my experience, those parents who respected their children's wishes and let go had a much better relationship with their children than did those parents who felt pressured by social patterns into taking custody.

D

DATING
(SEE ALSO *Adolescence, Independence, Individuality, Sex Education, Sexual Experiences*)

Dating is a fluctuating concept. In some communities teenagers no longer officially "date." They just "hang out" together. In others, children may begin to pair off at twelve or thirteen. The major questions of parents, when it comes to these situations, are very personal and best answered by parents themselves. However, I do think it is important that parents and teenagers discuss these issues openly in an attempt to work out what is appropriate, taking into account the parents' values and the values of the times, the values of the community, what the teenager's peers are doing, and the character of the individual adolescent. This does not mean that I think parents should allow a teenager to do whatever it is his friends are doing. But I do encourage parents to be somewhat flexible when dealing with adolescents, so that they can give them sufficient freedom to learn responsibility.

Many youngsters resent parents' insistence on knowing where they are going and with whom. However, if you have established an open and trusting relationship with your child, he will not view your questions as "nosiness" or "violations of privacy" but as genuine concern about his welfare. I certainly do not think it is unfair for parents to say, "Please call me if you are going to be late coming home." If your general attitude is compromising and friendly instead of strict or punitive, your youngster will be more inclined to do as you ask, without making an issue of it.

Some parents become distressed when their teenagers show a strong interest in the opposite sex. They think something must be wrong with their child, and view his life as "unbalanced." I don't think this is anything to be alarmed about. Each child develops in a unique fashion. If a child is happy, doing well in school, capable of enjoying friendships, and responsive to the emotional demands placed on him, then I would say his life seems balanced. I see nothing wrong with helping children learn the grooming habits and social graces that will aid them in the years ahead. But there is certainly no need to push a child into an interest in the opposite sex. I remember the response of one seemingly sophisticated ten-year-old boy who was being shown slides of the summer camp to which his parents were considering sending him. The camp director, who was showing the slides, repeatedly pointed out the pretty little girls. Finally, the boy spoke up: "Actually," he said, "I'm just *short* of puberty." As this little boy acknowledged, a child's interest in these matters will grow in its own time.

DAY CARE
(SEE ALSO *Babysitter, Family, Father, Mother*)

There are many parents who need to leave their young child in someone else's care for eight or nine hours a day, five days a week. For these people, I am a strong advocate of the best in child care.

Personally, I do not recommend leaving children under age three in an organized play situation with other children. When children are under three years of age they generally need a great deal of adult attention. For the most part, they're not ready for organized play with other children on a sustained basis. More often than not they tend to play by themselves, alongside other children, and frequently grab what they want when they want it. Since they also imitate the behavior of people around them, they frequently become more aggressive and show more destructive behavior if they've been in close contact for long periods of time with other children around two years of age. I don't mean to imply that on a child's third birthday he instantly and magically becomes a cooperative, trusting human being. But in general, three-year-olds are more capable of learning cooperative behavior, and are much better able to benefit from being in an organized play situation such as a nursery school. In fact, nursery school can be a very positive experience for a child of three years or more, and can help him learn to deal with peer situations.

Wherever small children are cared for all day—in a nursery school, day care center, child care facility, or private home—it would be wonderful if parents could spend lunch time with them. Not only would this give parents and children close contact with one another, it would serve to give the children the feeling that parents are important in their lives. When children spend little time with their parents, no matter how good the quality of time, the parents' importance in their children's lives is substantially diminished. I don't believe parents need to be with their children every minute of the day, but children do need to feel the presence and responsiveness of their parents for prolonged periods of time in the course of each day, particularly when they are very young. They need consistency, and they need to feel that their parents are important to them and they are important in the lives of their parents. If parents are gone for perhaps three or four hours at a time and return for an hour or two in between, their importance in their children's lives will be substantially greater than if they are gone for eight to nine hours a day at a stretch. If it's not possible for parents to return to their children at lunch time, perhaps whoever is caring for the children could bring them to one of the parents' workplaces for lunch.

When children are older and at school all day, it still may be that someone should be at home when the children return there after school. Many children who are capable of supervising themselves still need an adult at home to give them the feeling that there is someone who cares, can give them recognition, and can handle problems. Many children who come home to an empty house feel resentful; some feel sufficiently angry to be destructive. However, many other children not only are capable of doing without supervision, but are capable of handling family chores after school. This can give them a real sense of pride and accomplishment, and a feeling that they are important within the family, especially if parents show their appreciation for this kind of help.

I suggest that parents of school-age children discuss as a family the question of having an adult present after school. Parents could let their children know that they recognize that they're growing up and that perhaps there's little need to have someone take care of them for the few hours between the end of school and the parents' return from work. Parents should avoid pressuring their children, though, by giving them the impression that choosing to continue having an adult at home is a sign of immaturity.

There is every reason for parents to be responsive to their children's wishes and to let their children help them make this decision. This kind of family discussion can be a very positive experience for all family members; this kind of shared responsibility, shared decision-making, respect for one another's individuality and compassion for one another's needs is the best part of family life, and what makes a family a family instead of just a group of individuals who happen to be related and happen to share an environment. If both parents are at work all day, it can be particularly valuable for a family to come together in just this sort of activity.

DAYDREAMING
(SEE ALSO *Bashfulness, Boredom, Gifted Child, Imaginary Companions, Withdrawn Child*)

Constructing a world of their own in daydreams gives children the chance to try out different identities. In various fantasies a child can construct objects and relationships to test her ability to cope. Such fantasies are the result of a healthy, creative mind. I think parents can casually accept their child's "pretend" world, which shows respect for her feelings and ideas. At the same time, however, you should establish a difference between fantasy and reality. Otherwise, you may confuse the child into thinking her dream world *is* real! I see nothing wrong with a child's being engrossed in fantasies as long as she can relate to other people when necessary. If a child is *always* in her own world, and seems unable to interact socially, this may be due to boredom, or shyness, or fear of coping. The child who chronically daydreams, seems lost in another world, or finds it difficult to tell the difference between fantasy and reality may need professional help.

DEATH, IDEAS OF
(SEE ALSO *Funerals, Pets, Terminal Illness*)

Before the age of 2½ years, a child generally cannot understand the concept of death. Even by age four, death may not have any meaning unless someone she knows has suddenly "gone away." When a child becomes aware of death she will usually respond by asking, "Why can't the doctor fix him again?" "Where do dead people go?" "Will Uncle Brad come back?" "When will you die?" "When will I die?"

A child's curiosity about death can be difficult to deal with because she is trying to understand an abstract concept in concrete terms. Many adults have not come to grips with the topic themselves and so find it difficult to discuss.

I think you should answer your child's questions as honestly as you can, perhaps by saying initially that, "Aunt Elaine can't do things anymore because she is dead. Being dead is like being broken so that nobody can fix her—not even the doctors." It is very appropriate to express grief at this time, especially if the dead person was someone who was close to you and your child. You can say that everyone is very unhappy that Aunt Elaine died, and everybody will miss her.

It is psychologically as well as physically very healthy to express grief, as studies have shown. One doctor in Boston interviewed the families of victims of a large fire. The doctor found that the people who were dealing with their sorrow by expressing the greatest amount of grief had fewer psychosomatic reactions later on than those who showed little or no grief.

I cannot stress enough how important it is that you *not* equate death with going to sleep. Many parents tell their children that death is like "a long sleep." You can understand that the child who is told this will be afraid to go to sleep for fear that she will never wake up!

When a child confronts death for the first time, she may well be concerned about her own death. I think it is important to stress that she will not die for a very, very, long, long, long, long time. You can draw out the "long, long, long, long time" to assure your child that she is not going to die soon. She may also be concerned about the possible death of her parents. When a parent dies, very young children, say under five, view it as a separation. They may even have terrible guilt feelings if they think they were in some way responsible. (Every child may think, at some time or another, that her parent is mean and should go away.) The death of a parent is tragic for anyone, but especially for a young child who still very much needs that parental love and protection. There is really nothing that can ease the pain of a parental death, a sad fact that will shape one part of your child's reaction. She may also feel angry and resentful about having been "abandoned"—almost as if the parent actually chose to die and leave her. After all, children often believe that their parents are all-powerful and can do anything. So why didn't Mommy stay with us?

The surviving parent will need to offer a good deal of reassurance that he too is not going to leave. As the child is comforted she should be told it will probably take a long time to get over her unhappy feelings and in a way she will never really get completely over missing that person.

I think you should also tell your child that you know no one will ever replace that parent. Many parents take the misguided approach of telling the child that, "Your father is dead, but pretty soon you'll feel better and get over it." I think it is much wiser to acknowledge your child's feelings and allow her to discuss her feelings.

When the death of a sibling occurs, the child may believe that she will be next, since children often think events occur in a contiguous way. As I said before, I believe you should reassure your child that she is not going to die for a long, long time. A surviving sibling may also feel guilty if she thinks she has caused the death in any way. It is of the utmost importance to assure your child that she did nothing to cause the death, and that everyone did as much as possible to prevent it. Again, I think it is important to encourage your child to share her grief. Some parents try to remove all objects associated with the child who has died, but I believe that this conveys the notion that the dead person was not important enough to be remembered.

Possibly the most difficult situation to deal with is if a child actually is responsible in some way for someone's death. If such a tragedy occurs, it will do absolutely no good to add to the child's already tremendous burden of guilt by laying blame. The only thing you can do is try to continue assuring your child of your love, and to show compassion. Because any child would be scarred for life by such a situation, it is crucial that you never allow a child to be placed in a position where she might be responsible for anyone's death.

If a child is terminally ill and near death, I don't advise telling her so. For a further discussion of this topic, see TERMINAL ILLNESS.

DEFIANCE
(SEE ALSO *Adolescence, Bossiness, Discipline and Punishment, Disrespect, Independence, Individuality, Obedience, Rebellion, Stubbornness*)

Most children defy parental wishes from time to time; it's an expression of their individuality and quest for independence. Children are particularly defiant at certain ages. The list is headed by two-year-olds, whose favorite word is a resounding "No!", and adolescents, who, probably even at this moment, are slamming doors all across America. Four-year-olds would all like to be tyrants when they grow up. Such behavior is absolutely normal.

In fact, children who always comply with every parental wish may have certain emotional problems. Since they are extremely compliant they rarely show their own feelings. Among the main challenges of childhood is discovering one's self and expressing one's individuality as well as learning the structure and meaning of life. This is done by finding out about rules, regulations, and what causes things to happen. By acting defiantly, a child may be testing the limits, and testing his parents' reaction to what he does. This

63

kind of disobedience occurs from time to time and shouldn't be viewed by parents as a sign of emotional disturbance.

An example of normal defiance is the scene in the movie *Kramer vs. Kramer,* in which the father tells his son not to touch the ice cream, but the little boy continues to spoon it out of the carton until the father picks him up and physically prevents him from doing so. Another example of normal defiance is in Maurice Sendak's picture book, *Where the Wild Things Are.* Max, the hero, does something mischievous, and his mother calls him a "wild thing." Defiantly, Max shouts back, "I'll eat you up!" so he's sent to his room without his supper. He then imagines that he sails off to "where the wild things are" and is crowned king. But the important thing is that Max doesn't want to *stay* "where the wild things are." He doesn't want to be defiant all the time—just once in a while, to test the limits. So he goes home, and happily finds his supper, which is even still hot.

However, when a child wants to *stay* "where the wild things are" —when he *always* does the opposite of what his parents ask, this reflects a problem in the parent-child relationship. Children who defy every wish may be saying they are angry and resentful of their parents' authority. Perhaps they feel their wishes have been ignored or their parents have been dictatorial. In order for your child to respect your wishes, ideas, rules, and regulations, it is important for you to show respect for your child's individuality, and to recognize his own wishes and desires—even if you cannot comply with them. When parents are too demanding and set severe limits on their children's freedom, children are inclined to be defiant of any rules that are set up. But when there is open, trusting communication between parents and children it is less likely that children will continually disobey.

Constant misbehavior may have another cause: Some children, because of severe conflicts, may be expressing a need for help through disturbed or defiant behavior.

Other children who always misbehave may be in need of attention. I have worked with many children who come from homes where their parents are preoccupied with their own problems, or for a variety of other reasons pay little attention to their children. Only when their children are in trouble or have serious problems do these parents seem to pay attention to them. Not surprisingly, these children learn rather quickly that they can get attention if they manage to create problems. To a child, even negative attention is better than being ignored.

I cannot stress enough the importance of a child's need for positive attention and acceptance from the significant adults in his life. This, above all, will help counteract acts of defiance. Children need reinforcement for showing socially acceptable behavior. With parental love, attention, and support, children will learn to care about other people's feelings. They can also learn that rules and regulations are not meant as deprivation, but as protection and support.

DEPRESSION
(SEE ALSO *Adolescence, Babysitter, Boredom, Crying, Fear, Infancy, Neurosis, Separation Anxiety, Sleep, Suicide, Travel, Withdrawn Child*)

When a child is depressed she is most often suffering from what is known as "reactive depression"—a response to circumstances in her life.

Even infants can feel depressed. The depressed infant will sometimes stare into space, whine, or show generally lethargic behavior. Such depression can be caused by lack of stimulation, lack of cuddling, or crying for long periods of time. Depression in infants can also occur when parents go away and leave the child with someone else—for example, when they go off on vacation. If you are going on vacation, I recommend that you take your child with you until she is two years old, or until she is verbal enough to understand the difference between "today," "tomorrow," and "the next day." It is important that your child be able to understand when you are going and when you are coming back. Otherwise, the child may feel a sense of loss and abandonment. She may refuse food. This depression doesn't last forever. The child does get over it. But the child may develop anxiety, clinging behavior, and/or sleep difficulties—the idea being, "If I go to sleep it may cause my parents to go away again."

Depression can occur in early to middle childhood when parents are overly critical of a child, or set high standards that the child is unable to achieve. Often, these children manifest their depression by just "giving up," showing poor motivation, and isolating themselves.

Depression is common during adolescence, because of the many changes that take place. Teenagers are in search of an identity, and are very sensitive to any possible rejection. However, if a teenager's depression persists, if it interferes with her ability to maintain social relations and to keep up with her responsibilities in school, you should take this situation very seriously. The adolescent suicide rate is very high. Do seek professional help.

DISCIPLINE AND PUNISHMENT
(SEE ALSO *Acceptance, Adolescence, Approval, Behavior Modification, Bribery, Conscience, Grandparents, Model Child, Praise, Rewards, Spanking, Toilet Training*)

To begin with, I would like to distinguish between discipline and punishment. To my mind, discipline means establishing rules and regulations of behavior that are set up to protect the integrity and the rights of others. I see discipline as being an element in showing love for a child.

Discipline involves a discernible, consistent pattern, a framework of rules within which a child can function with a sense of predictability. We all have a desire to be able to predict the future. If we feel as though we know what is likely to happen in our lives, we feel less anxiety and a greater degree of security.

If no rules of behavior are established for a child—or if those rules are ambiguous—that youngster will probably be anxious and perhaps destructive, not out of hostility, but because he is asking someone to set limits. Instituting discipline is a continuation of your love and concern for your child. It shows you care. Now that your child is growing and interacting with the rest of the world, you need to help him learn how to cope with his curiosity about his environment. In this way he will be able to direct his interests outside himself so that he won't function just in terms of his own impulses without regard for other people's feelings. By establishing rules for your child you will have equipped him with the ability to deal with many of the situations that occur in life.

The most effective people to discipline a child are those in whom he has a sense of trust, those who have offered him protection and satisfied his needs. Since parents are generally the people for whom the child has these feelings most strongly, they are generally the ones who are the most effective disciplinarians. When a child knows his parents love him, he has a strong inclination to follow the rules in order to preserve that love. When you express pleasure and pride in your child's behavior, you will be reinforcing it. On the other hand, expressing annoyance, dissatisfaction, and rejection of behavior makes it clear that you disapprove. In this way, you guide your child's behavior.

Parents who spend little time with their children or who provide little satisfaction of their needs early in life are not as effective in setting rules and regulations later on. After all, why should a child care about his parents' reactions if they have never shown any particular concern about his needs?

Most children will periodically test the rules and regulations you set. For this reason you must be consistent. Similarly, you must enforce whatever punishment you have established for violation of the rules. Threatening a child with punishment and not carrying it out weakens your credibility and makes your child anxious that you do not care about his behavior, and intensifies his need to be certain that you mean what you say. I find that when parents are inconsistent in this way, children tend to be more defiant of rules and regulations. It's almost as if they are saying to the parent, "Please show me that you are consistent—I don't believe you are going to carry out your threats or promises." In a way, they are hoping you will show the strength of your convictions. A parent who means what he or she says, provides a child with a greater feeling of security.

Mothers and fathers may not always agree on all aspects of a child's discipline and punishment, but it is extremely important that one not undermine the authority of the other. When parents contradict each other on a disciplinary matter, the child is left feeling vulnerable and insecure because of the inconsistencies he encounters.

Even if the father, for example, disagrees with the rules set by the mother, it is best if he temporarily supports her position. Later, both can talk it over in private and if they agree to change the rules or the punishment, that parent, in this case the mother, who set the rule in the first place should be the one to inform the child of the change. This will prevent the child from trying to manipulate the parents or to play one against the other.

I want to reiterate that discipline and punishment are best administered by a child's parents. One of the disadvantages of having many different people care for your child is that often they have different expectations from you with regard to the child's behavior. While an older child may benefit from learning to respond to various people and situations, a young child who is just learning to do things for himself will have to shift gears when different people take over. This is not to say you shouldn't leave a child with a sitter, a friend, or a relative sometimes, but you should try to ensure a certain consistency for the child. Those who do take care of him should be taught your approach.

When you set guidelines for your child, evaluate his capabilities, not his chronological age. When he begins to move around in his environment, he starts to reach for things and is able to grasp them and push or pull them. This is when you have to let him know what is acceptable behavior and what is not.

I don't believe in removing everything from the coffee table or rearranging your home so that everything is out of a toddler's reach; this doesn't solve the problem, it only avoids the issue. You are also limiting your child's learning by not allowing him to explore. I would suggest that you take away especially fragile things that can be easily broken, and then set conditions as to the other possessions that he can and cannot touch. This is called baby-proofing the home.

The rules and regulations you establish and enforce should be set at a level that he can understand. Thus, while it is quite possible to teach an eight- or nine-month-old that it is all right to tear newspapers but not magazines, it is not possible to teach him that he can tear yesterday's paper, but not today's. That would be too much to expect, since he hasn't learned to read words or recognize dates.

If you are surprised that a child of less than a year old can be taught not to tear magazines, while he is allowed to destroy newspapers, let me explain how it's done. You may allow your child to approach a coffee table piled with magazines and newspapers. In all likelihood your child may begin to play with them and will look at you as he explores the piles to discover your reaction. As he begins to tear a magazine, take it away, say "No" very firmly, and emphatically express your annoyance so that your displeasure is clearly understood. Now hand the magazine back to him. More than likely he will make another attempt to tear the magazine, and you should again react in exactly the same way. Then your child will begin to see the consistent pattern in your behavior. He will probably want to test your reaction several times. At some point you can pick up a newspaper, tear it and then show your child that he may tear the newspaper. If you are going to teach him not to tear magazines, you will have to allow time and exercise much patience if he is to learn all of what you want him to understand.

Attempting to reason with a toddler can only lead to frustration, because children under three generally have difficulty understanding such reasoning. Your disapproving look or firm tone of voice will probably be sufficient. (Sometimes you must be very firm, especially where your young child's safety is concerned.) But you can forewarn an older child. In this way you are really giving the child a certain amount of freedom, rather than making him feel powerless and uncertain.

I believe spanking is psychologically harmful and I'm against it. Indeed, children who are often brutalized grow up to be hostile or destructive adults. Whenever a punishment exceeds the severity of the misbehavior, your child will see you as mean and not protective. As much as possible, the severity should fit the crime. Depriving a child of playing a very important baseball game he has looked forward to, because he didn't brush his teeth in the morning may be too severe and is also inappropriate. Not brushing one's teeth is hardly an infraction that merits missing an important game, and playing baseball has nothing to do with brushing teeth.

Punishment can also be detrimental if it has no proximity in time to the misbehavior. For example, if a child disregards a rule, it is unfair to deprive him of going to the circus three months in the future. Such a punishment is too far removed.

Parents sometimes think they can help a child overcome a problem through shaming him in front of friends, teachers, or family members. This is what parents sometimes do to a child who bites his nails, wets his bed, or is a poor eater. It is a form of humiliation, which is meant to cause a child sufficiently strong unpleasant feelings to make the behavior stop. While it may accomplish this immediate goal, the long-range damage far exceeds the apparent immediate benefits. I strongly disapprove of ever using shame, not only with children but with anyone. It is demeaning, can injure self-esteem, cause strong anger and resentment, and perhaps even precipitate an emotional problem that can last throughout a person's life.

When punishment is appropriate it helps a child internalize values, and preserves his self-esteem. To do this you must remember to take into consideration his feelings and let him know you understand him. You can accomplish this by consulting your children about the appropriateness of punishment when they violate the rules. For example, explain to your child, "I warned you that I would have to punish you if you did it again—you did, and now we have to decide upon a punishment. What do *you* think a reasonable punishment would be for what you've done?" More often than not, children recommend a punishment that is extremely severe: "Don't feed me for a month." Or "Don't let me out of the house for a year." You can then continue to negotiate by saying, "That's too harsh. Think of another one." Ultimately you can arrive at a punishment.

By working it out with your child you are not only enforcing the rule, but you are being compassionate in not wanting to be too severe, and you are also taking into consideration the child's wishes and feelings, and showing respect for him.

One final note. Giving a child a present as a reward for acceptable behavior and taking things away as punishment simply places the emphasis on the material objects and not on his behavior. It makes the object more important than it should be. The rewards I recommend are your feelings and reactions to your child's behavior. Using affection and acceptance teaches that rewards in life come from human interaction and not material goods.

DISRESPECT
(SEE ALSO *Adolescence, Defiance, Discipline and Punishment*)

Young children can often be momentarily rude, but I don't think this means they are being disrespectful. If, in a fit of anger, a child yells at his parents "You're so stupid!" he is probably just expressing temporary frustration. You can let your child know that you don't approve of this kind of talk, but I don't believe the remark warrants punishment. True disrespect is a much more consistent rejection of authority, and is an expression of underlying hostility in a child. Such antisocial behavior is a signal that the child wants and needs more discipline. If parents are consistent in their discipline and punishment of a child, the youngster is more apt to stay comfortable within the limits that have been set and be more respectful of other people's rights and feelings. The chronically disrespectful child is harboring unhappiness and frustration, most likely directed at his parents. If parents cannot uncover and correct the source of that frustration, I strongly recommend seeking professional advice.

DIVORCE
(SEE ALSO *Arguments Between Parents, Custody, Father, Mother, Stepparent*)

Divorce is often an anguishing experience for children as well as for parents. It is almost always an upheaval, because it usually involves many changes. However, I have seen very few children irrevocably damaged as a result. In fact, many children whose parents are divorced emerge stronger and with more understanding of life and relationships than their contemporaries. As they grow up, many say they still consider marriage the best lifestyle, but they want to make certain they know themselves and the other person well before making such an important commitment. These children learn about what a marriage really involves, and may actually be more sensitive to the need for making relationships work.

Often it is not the divorce itself, but the problems leading up to it, and the indignities caused by some aspects of the legal process, that are responsible for the later difficulties of children. If the children's feelings and rights are respected by parents and the legal system, they can learn from a divorce that it is possible to resolve a painful human conflict. They can learn that solutions can be worked out, and that difficulty can lead to positive ends. I am not saying that divorce is good for your child. I am only pointing out that divorce is not inevitably harmful to your child if it is dealt with in a manner that protects the child's integrity and approaches the issues constructively.

Based on my experience, most children of divorced parents would have been far worse off if their parents had remained together in a strained, loveless, or embattled marriage. It is vitally important for children to see parents in a loving relationship. This serves as a model for a child of what a caring relationship is like. If a marriage cannot work, the parents and children would all be better off if the parents became free to find loving relationships elsewhere. As one child of divorced parents put it, "Though everyone is always saying divorce hurts the children, in the old days when people *didn't* divorce, the (tension) hurt the children even more. Sometimes divorce is better than having to put rock music on so loud you can't hear your parents fighting with each other. . . ." I have had many adult patients who told me that as children they couldn't wait to leave home because of family tensions or the absence of spontaneous affection between their parents. They've said, "I wish my parents had divorced and found happiness in other relationships." Other patients whose parents had divorced admitted that it was difficult for a while, but in the long run "we were all better off."

Sometimes parents with unsatisfactory marriages try to sustain them with a minimum of friction through a minimum of interaction. In such households there is no authentic family unit or affection, only a kind of "truce" or "coexistence." What concerns me about these arrangements is that often the children of such households seek out a substitute for family life—a peer group, gang, or cult of some sort. In my view, these children, and many, many others I've seen in my professional practice whose parents chose to avoid divorce to "protect the children," would have been better off if their parents had faced the trauma of divorce, dealt with it effectively, and worked toward a potentially more gratifying life.

Children are far more capable of understanding divorce than many parents realize. A child whose parents are open and frank feels far less responsible for family problems than the child whose parents attempt to conceal the gravity of the situation. Parents who claim they remain together "for the sake of the children" are not helping their youngsters: they are clinging to the relationship for their own reasons, placing a dishonest and unfair burden on the children, and denying the children the model of either a loving relationship or of parents who can face their difficulties, deal with them, and learn from them.

There is no particular age when children will adjust best to a divorce. It all depends on the individual family and the individual child. It's best if both mother and father explain the divorce to the child—without, however, turning it into an argument. The explanation should be tailored to fit the child's age and understanding. But whatever the circumstances of the divorce, parents should emphasize that they were both disappointed that things didn't work out the way they wanted them to—even if one parent is bitterly opposed to the divorce. The idea is for you to help your child deal with his emotions at this time, and you only complicate matters if you inject your own. If you have had an open and trusting relationship with your child up to this point, your child will be able to express his feelings and to ask you questions.

Typically, one of the first reactions a child has to divorce is to ask, "What did I do (or not do) that caused this?" A little girl I recently saw said, "I think the reason my daddy went away was that he wanted to kiss me one night and I was too busy reading a book." *A child has to be reassured that he has absolutely no responsibility for the breakup of the marriage*. Children's reactions to the announcement of divorce vary, but a child who shows no emotion is nevertheless reacting—he may be in a state of shock, or he may need time to think before responding.

If one parent plans to remarry immediately after the divorce, the children may understandably demonstrate resentment. It's difficult enough for them to adjust to the divorce itself, without this additional change; and they will be predisposed to look upon the new spouse as the cause of the divorce, which can make them view that person negatively. It's best to wait before introducing a new person into their lives.

Often, tension and conflict remain after a divorce because of inappropriate living arrangements. In the entry on "Custody" I discuss my belief that the concept of "custody" implies ownership, and children as prizes or property, which sets up an adversary relationship between parents. Rather than "custody," I would prefer to substitute the idea of "responsibility." In my opinion, children's feelings about whom they would rather live with are very important, and should be drawn out and carefully considered. But children themselves should not make the decision about custody. That should be left to the parents or the legal authorities involved. Unfortunately, many of the people who make decisions involving "custody" and "visitation" do so in a way that makes it easier for adults, not best for children. Once mothers and fathers have equal custody rights, the best interests of the child can be evaluated more rationally. Part of the present problem is that mothers are reluctant to relinquish care of the children to fathers for fear that they will be denounced. The more truly liberated we become, the more the responsibility for raising a child will fall on the parent who is better able to fulfill that responsibility.

As far as so-called joint custody goes, it's not necessarily in the best interest of the child to be shared arbitrarily and artificially with alternate weeks spent at each parent's house. Rather, it should mean that the parents share equal *responsibility* for making decisions involving the education, health, and well-being of the child. This, of course, requires that parents be able to cooperate on such matters.

Some other problems associated with divorce may occur because parents let out their frustrations about the divorce on their child, or exploit their child for emotional support, which is a great burden. Occasionally parents may try to use a child to check up on the former spouse, or as a sounding board for grievances. One little girl was upset because all she heard from her mother was what a terrible person her father was. I had to help her get to the point where she could tell her mother, "It's your divorce, not mine. You're angry with my daddy and I love him. I just don't want to hear any more about it."

I don't advocate divorce unless every possible attempt has been made to work out problems within the marriage. But when problems cannot be worked out in this way, divorce is a reasonable and necessary process that may enable both people to continue and to grow. Divorce can lead to further growth for children, too, if parents protect their child's integrity and deal with the issues constructively.

DOCTOR/MEDICAL EXAMINATION
(SEE ALSO *Hospitalization, Illness, Terminal Illness*)

About a day before your child is scheduled for a routine visit to the doctor or dentist, you should tell him you are taking him and why, and what he can expect. A child's apprehension about visits to the doctor usually starts when the doctor begins to do strange things that are unpleasant. Having strange instruments stuck in his ears, nose, and mouth, being pricked with needles, and having someone poking around where it sometimes hurts is not only unpleasant, it is an infringement of privacy and an intrusion on his free will. If the child were more familiar with what was going on, he would be less scared. While I think it is important to prepare your child for what will occur, I think it is equally important not to overprepare him by going into more detail than he needs. Don't be overly serious or morose. That will serve to increase his anxiety.

Once at the doctor's office, you should lend emotional support if your child becomes frightened and apprehensive. For instance, if he is about to be given a shot, you can tell him matter-of-factly: "The doctor must give you a shot and it may hurt a bit, but he will do it quickly and get it over with." Don't mislead him by saying, "This won't hurt a bit." When it does, he will not only resent everyone involved, but will feel deceived and deprived of his capacity for using his own resources for coping. By preparing him for what will happen, and acknowledging that it may hurt (and that it is all right to cry), you are showing respect for his feelings and allowing him to mobilize his resources to deal with the situation. This enhances his self-esteem and makes him feel that he has come through an unpleasant procedure with an awareness of what happened.

If a doctor misleads your child, do not take sides with the doctor. If you do, you weaken your child's confidence in you by defending a doctor your child sees as dishonest. I can remember being lied to when I was six years old on my first visit to a dentist. He said, "Open your mouth and let me look, I'm not going to do anything." When I opened my mouth he put his fingers inside and pulled out two of my loose teeth. To this day, I can hear those teeth hit the floor and I can remember the taste of blood. And even now when I visit the dentist I want to be told in advance everything that could happen. I'm sure my present dentist is the unfortunate target of the anger I felt for that first dentist. A trusting relationship with a doctor or dentist is basic to the development of proper health habits. For that reason, if you are dissatisfied with your doctor's techniques in dealing with children, you might consider finding a more sensitive doctor.

Another technique that can be very helpful to your child is giving him some control over the painful situation and letting him feel that he has some choice in the matter. You can ask him "Would you like your injection while you're standing up—or while you're sitting down?" or "Would you like your injection in this arm or that arm?" or "Would you like a green lollipop or a red one?" These choices may seem relatively unimportant to you but they give your child the feeling that he is participating in his fate. Giving your child a choice notifies him that you are concerned about him. Even though you are asking him to undergo something unpleasant you still want to make it as agreeable as possible. After all, he is not in a position to choose whether the treatment will be done or not. The choice has been made for him. So at least give him the opportunity of choosing within reasonable limits how it is to be done. If your child refuses to make the choice, you will have to make it for him. But even then you have conveyed the idea that you are concerned with his feelings and are on record as having given him a choice.

Since you can't prepare an infant or a young baby for a physical examination or some other unpleasant procedure, you can at least buffer the unpleasantness by holding and cuddling your child. Communicate sympathy in any way you can, or try to distract your infant with a toy or a lollipop.

DRINKING
(SEE ALSO *Alcohol and Drug Abuse Among Teenagers, Smoking*)

Children who are exposed to an adult with a drinking problem are bound to ask questions, and when they do, it's time to explain about alcoholism. You can say that some people drink too much because they are unhappy about themselves. They may start out drinking very little just to relax, but as time goes on, they need to drink more and more; then they can't seem to stop themselves, even though they realize that drinking so much can be very harmful to them. Explain that when people drink a lot, it makes them feel strange and do strange things.

Let your children know some of the hazards that can occur when a person is drunk—that people who drink too much can be dangerous when they drive or may become so uncoordinated that they may hurt themselves or others. While this may frighten children somewhat, it will help them understand the consequences when a person is unable to control his or her impulses. I think it's fair to add that many people drink occasionally when they celebrate special events, or before mealtimes at the end of a hard day, because it makes them feel happier and more relaxed. Emphasize the fact that people who drink a lot, and have become alcoholics are not necessarily bad people, but merely people who require understanding and help so that they can overcome their problems.

Treat your children's questions with respect, and make sure that their curiosity is satisfied. In this way you will be helping them understand alcoholism and give them valuable knowledge to guard against their getting caught up in such a problem themselves later on.

Some parents allow their preteen child to sip from a glass of champagne, beer, or wine on special occasions such as weddings. Some adults may react with shock and dismay to this scene, others may smile and pronounce the child "adorable." In my experience, when parents take a strongly prohibitive view of alcohol, they tend to make it seem more enticing and drinking it adventurous. On the other hand, seeing its consumption by a child as cute and charming can also make it enticing. In either case, it can increase the child's motivation to drink alcohol. The moment you offer attention, either positive or negative, you are giving alcohol a value that goes beyond a matter of simple curiosity about taste, and you can thus intensify your child's desire for this experience. Your child may use drinking alcohol as a means of defying you, hurting you, or showing his independence. A casual attitude is best; in all likelihood, if you handle the matter nonchalantly, the desire will diminish.

DROPPING THINGS
(SEE ALSO *Infancy, Learning, Play*)

Babies become fascinated with dropping things to the floor, usually while sitting in a high chair or in a crib. It starts when they learn to hold and release objects, and usually occurs by accident. Your response will probably be to bend over, pick up the object, and give it back to her. She will be amazed by this new-found accomplishment. With a simple movement of her hand, she has lightened her load, changed your posture, and caused you to retrieve the object. No wonder she's fascinated and wants to repeat this behavior, seemingly interminably. She has now learned that she can do things to her environment that make it change substantially. You may well think your child is trying to make your life difficult, by dropping her toy repeatedly to see whether you will pick it up. But to your child, who is beginning to explore how things work in the world around her, she is gaining a great sense of accomplishment by learning to control her environment. In the process, she begins to feel a greater sense of security about her surroundings.

In all likelihood your child will continue to drop her toy a number of times until she is convinced that dropping leads to a predictable set of events. After she has fully explored the matter of gravity, and knows that objects of all sorts go down and not up, her curiosity will be partly satisfied.

However, it's important for her to learn that it is permissible to drop some things and not others. It's also important for her to learn that you may become irritated if this activity continues indefinitely. If, for example, she attempts to spill her milk, you may in a firm, annoyed voice, say "No." At the same time, remove the milk and substitute perhaps a rubber toy or some paper crushed into a ball, and let her drop that. You can show your approval of her dropping certain objects by smiling, and your disapproval of other objects by a firm "No" and an unfriendly frown.

F

FAMILY
(SEE ALSO *Allowance, Child Abuse, Childbirth, Custody, Day Care, Divorce, Father, Grandparents, Listening, Mother*)

The family is the key social unit within which human beings develop the skills for being able to cope with life's problems. It is only through feeling important to at least one other person in the course of early growth and development that we can learn how to love. It is only through this same early attachment to at least one other person that we can gain a sense of self-worth sufficient to make us a useful member of society.

We have been inclined to think of the family in structural terms —as a mother, father, and perhaps two children. I prefer to think of it in functional terms. I have known many families that are structurally intact but do not function as a family. Each member goes about his or her own business, hardly communicating with one another, showing little or no interest in what is going on in the others' lives. There are few mutual decisions, there is little cooperative activity. On the other hand, I have known of many single-parent families that function as a strong family unit, where each family member plays an important role in the life of the other, and where there is deep concern about the feelings of the other.

Whether we think of the family in structural or functional terms, we must acknowledge the stresses on family life today. The major problem now facing families is that family members seem to have less and less time to spend with one another. Far less parental time is available to children. With the little time families *do* have together, many of them spend a considerable percentage of it in front of a television screen. At the same time the family's values are heavily influenced by the material on the screen, the family members are losing touch with one another. Many parents who have little time to spend with their children feel guilty about this. They recognize the shortcomings in any substitute for a strong, meaningful, caring relationship between a child and a parent.

In the future, I hope there will be changes that will enable working parents to have enough flexibility to meet their children's emotional needs. Flexible working hours, job sharing, and family travel together on business trips might be among these changes.

The family is so important for healthy human development that I think every effort should be made to preserve it. If the family as a unit were to disintegrate, it would have very serious negative consequences for the future of our civilization.

FATHER
(SEE ALSO *Childbirth, Custody, Day Care, Divorce, Mother, Oedipus Complex*)

A father or father substitute is essential to the emotional development of both boys and girls. For boys, the father is the main model of masculinity—of what it means to be a man, father, husband. For girls, the father is a model for all men; their later relationships with boys and men will be influenced by their relationships with their fathers.

In a sense, fathers have been ignored, but that is changing and is a trend for the better, in my opinion. I feel quite strongly that fatherhood has many rewards and satisfactions; equally importantly, fatherhood provides the opportunity to influence the development of a new life.

When my son Eric was born twenty years ago, and I became a father for the first time, I wanted desperately to be present in the delivery room, but this was automatically prohibited in hospitals at that time. I was considered peculiar even to make the request. The best I could manage, after pressuring and cajoling the authorities was to be present in the labor room. Immediately after Eric's birth, before he was bathed, I was given permission to see him. His eyes were wide open and he was very alert. We had direct eye-to-eye contact, and I will never forget the intensity of my emotions at that moment and the strong feeling of bonding it created in me.

Right from birth, I became intimately involved in the rearing of my son. On weekdays, when most fathers were at work, I would spend hours with my toddler at a playground in Central Park. I couldn't help noticing the questioning looks that mothers, nurse-maids, and babysitters gave me. I knew they must be wondering: Why isn't this man working? Is he unemployed? Where is his wife? Without a doubt, this was not what fathers were expected to do. Only a few years later, I was asked to write an article about father-hood for a leading family magazine. Since the article was to be the lead story, I asked the editor to do what I had never seen done before: put a father on the cover holding a baby. In that article, I presented an argument in support of fathers taking a strong nurtur-ant role in the care of their children, since I believed that males had a deep desire to actively participate in child rearing.

Today, much to my satisfaction, fathers are encouraged to take classes with their wives to prepare for childbirth and to be present in labor and delivery rooms. Birthing rooms are becoming common in hospitals, allowing families to be together during this momentous occasion.

We hear not only of fathers sharing equally in child rearing, but of househusbands, who take care of household duties while mothers work outside the home. (One famous proponent of househusbandry was John Lennon, who took care of his son Sean during the day while his wife, Yoko Ono, handled their business affairs.)

The question of the father being considered a legitimate parent is no longer even an issue. Fathers fight for child custody, and even win. In the early stages of my career, when I addressed fathers on how to give love and discipline to their children, I was likely to be told by them, "That's my wife's responsibility." Today, I see fa-thers playing a significant part in the everyday lives of their chil-dren.

There is no reason why fathers and mothers cannot do the same things to care for their children. Both fathers and mothers can support children financially. Both mothers and fathers can feed, bathe, rock, dress, change the diapers of and play peek-a-boo with their babies. Both fathers and mothers can read books, take walks, sing songs, bake cookies, and build block towers with their small children. Both can play Monopoly, Scrabble, checkers, chess, pinochle, poker, baseball, and football with their school-age children; they can help them with their homework and take them to the doctor and the dentist and their music or dancing or karate lessons. Both fathers and mothers can have long talks with their teenagers about art, music, literature, sports, politics, and sex. Both can have vociferous disagreements with their teenagers about art, music, literature, sports, politics, and sex—and anything else under the sun. Both fathers and mothers can go fishing, ice skating, and boating with their teenagers, or to movies, museums, pizza parlors, art galleries, lakes, or bowling alleys. Both mothers and fathers can serve as role models for their children, discipline their children, hug and kiss and cuddle and talk with and listen to and love their children.

As I have said elsewhere, I believe that being a parent—father *or* mother—is the most important role a person can assume. It is my conviction that both mothers and fathers can take an equal part in the most challenging and fulfilling experience in life—raising a child to fulfill his potential as a person.

FEARS
(SEE ALSO *Neurosis*)

Some fears are a natural, normal part of childhood. After all, children are small and inexperienced in the world. It is understandable if they have a somewhat primitive response to an experience such as lightning or thunder or a big, barking dog. Fear of the dark is quite common in young children, as is fear of the dentist, fear of fire, fear of airplanes, and the more basic fear of abandonment.

If your child says he is afraid to go to sleep at night because there are monsters under his bed, or that he doesn't want to go next door because there is a beast in the backyard, you should respect your child's fear and help him work through it by providing every opportunity for him to talk about it with you. It is not at all useful to force him to squarely confront his fear. Above all, do not ridicule him, as this is sure to make him feel like a failure, and will also make him resentful of you.

The important thing to remember here is, no matter how sure you are that the monster is imaginary, no matter how certain you are that the beast is a German shepherd, the monster is real to your child, and the dog is beastly. All the reasoning in the world won't change this. When your child cries out in fear, he needs your comfort and compassion. He needs you to help him deal with his feelings about the monster and the beast rather than your attempt to convince him that the monster and the beast aren't real.

As far as a night light is concerned, if it helps a child to sleep more comfortably and feel less frightened, I see no reason not to use one. Even many adults like a little light somewhere in the room when they go to sleep, if only to help them become oriented should they wake suddenly at night.

A phobia is basically a severe anxiety reaction set off by certain objects or situations that realistically cause little or no actual danger —and yet a person's response can be overwhelming, and can cause intense and crippling anxiety. It is true that some phobias are somewhat appropriate and not without a certain basis in fact. Some people are phobic about elevators, and after all, on occasion people do get stuck on elevators. Some people are phobic about flying, and it is true airplanes do now and then crash. However, phobias are such fears grown out of proportion, when anxiety becomes incapacitating. If a person is not able to move freely in circumstances where elevator travel is essential, the problem would not just be a simple fear of elevator travel, it would be a phobia.

Occasionally phobias develop following a real-life experience, such as falling from a horse or being in an automobile accident. Usually they are not set off by a literal experience, but have a rather deep psychological significance. Phobias result because a person at some time or another had a very strong impulse to express a feeling or do something that was highly unacceptable to his conscience. In an attempt to place distance between himself and that forbidden impulse, the human mind reacts with a series of emotional mechanisms. The mind represses the impulse altogether and does its best to deny that it even happened, or blames it on someone or something else, or takes the person toward whom that unacceptable impulse was meant and displaces those feelings onto something else. The phobia is to some extent the end product of all the intricate psychological mechanisms that people use to protect themselves from expressing an unacceptable impulse toward someone they love or depend on. In general, once established, phobias persist and sometimes get worse as those repressed impulses continue to build up. If this happens, professional psychological help is necessary. Children will not pick up a specific phobia from parents or relatives unless the children have certain underlying emotional weaknesses themselves. On the other hand, they can develop some anxiety when they see a parent panic, since children need to feel that their parents have sufficient stability and control to help *them* with their fears and problems.

Sometimes parents report that their child has a phobia, when it is in fact a straightforward, realistic, legitimate fear. For example, I have had many children referred to me for "school phobias." Actually these children have merely had perfectly rational reactions to frightening experiences—a bully lying in wait for them on the way to school, or an overbearing teacher. I can remember having a fourth grade teacher who frightened me so with her screaming that I got sick to my stomach every day before school. The sick feeling disappeared as soon as I changed to the next grade.

If your child's fears do not disappear, however, but seem deep and persistent, and not really related to any actual experience, I recommend that you take your child to a licensed, certified psychologist or psychiatrist to uncover the underlying emotional problem.

FOOD, SYMBOLIC AS REWARD AND/OR PUNISHMENT
(SEE ALSO *Anorexia Nervosa, Appetite, Breastfeeding, Drinking, Neurosis, Obesity, Smoking, Sucking, Weaning*)

Aside from the physical need for food, there is a certain amount of emotional satisfaction in eating. The gratification that an infant gets while feeding is primarily associated with satisfying her sucking needs. How much food is consumed is actually secondary. Studies have shown that frustration of this early sucking need can lead to an adult who overeats to fulfill an emotional craving. (That same adult might also smoke or drink excessively to find gratification of oral needs in some indirect way.) Food can also become linked with relieving boredom or reducing stress. But overeating has only temporary rewards: while it tastes good it can lead to obesity, which can lead to ridicule, unhappiness, and depression. This can send a person back to food in order to feel good. It is a cycle that can be hard to break.

When this occurs, we are confronted with the problem of compulsive eating, that is, an apparent inability to control the impulse to eat. I think one of the best ways to prevent this problem is to avoid using food as a reward. Giving a child a sweet or dessert for being "good" can condition her to think of food as an expression of love. Parents frequently say to their children, "You'll feel better if you eat something," or "If you behave yourself, I'll give you some candy." This causes food to become an expression of love and parental acceptance. It reinforces the idea that food, instead of human interaction, is the greatest source of emotional satisfaction.

Perhaps unwittingly, parents can give food exaggerated importance when they withhold it as a punishment. Sending a child to bed without any dinner can convey the message that denying food is tantamount to denying approval and hence denying love. This may seem like a rather convoluted association, but in the mind of the child being punished in this way, food becomes symbolic of love withheld. Aside from feeling hurt and resentful (not to mention hungry!) the child sent to her room without dinner may well come to use food as a substitute for emotional satisfaction later in life. She may try to "recapture" the love that was at one time denied, and when she feels unloved may develop an overwhelming impulse to eat, only to find that the need is insatiable, because food can never provide the satisfaction that comes from sincere parental love.

FRIENDS
(SEE ALSO *Club, Gang, Withdrawn Child*)

By making friends, the schoolchild expands her world outside the family and learns the joys of communicating and sharing with other people her own age. Her friends can relate to her fears, frustrations, and delights because they, too, are living through these experiences.

The need for friends becomes even more important as children approach adolescence. A growing interest in the opposite sex poses many dilemmas that teenagers need to discuss with one another. In this way they learn that they are not the only ones who feel "weird," and this is indeed a comforting reassurance.

I often hear parents express concern about some of the company their children keep. Understandably, parents are sometimes worried that their child will come under a "bad influence" if she plays with "troublemakers" or with children who are raised with a different set of values.

As a general rule, I believe it is unwise to interfere with your child's choice of playmates. If you demand that she stop seeing a certain friend she will probably react in one of two extreme ways: she will either comply with your wish, await your stamp of approval on other friends and hesitate to assert herself independently in relationships; or she will rebel and sneak away to play with the forbidden friend, all the while harboring resentment toward you.

I think it is best to simply help your child cope in her relationships with others by providing guidance and support when problems arise.

It is not unusual for children to limit their peer group to one person—a "best friend." I see absolutely nothing wrong with a child's focusing her interest on one friend rather than spreading herself among many. She and her friend are probably sufficiently compatible to meet each other's needs at a particular time. Many of us can remember having a best friend during childhood—a friendship we thought would last forever. Yet, inevitably, another person comes along and takes that friend's place. In all likelihood your child will develop other friendships in time.

Still other children are relatively isolated socially and this can be due to many factors. A shy child may avoid contact with people because she lacks the social skills to interact. As I mentioned above, some children whose parents have tried to pick their friends lose faith in their own judgment and do not assert themselves socially. If your child is isolated, you can help her become involved with friends by promoting participation in groups and expressing confidence that she can do so. Encourage her to interact by offering a friendly hello and engaging other children in conversation. If your child observes you taking part in groups, she will be able to emulate you.

FUNERALS, TAKING CHILDREN TO
(SEE ALSO *Death, Ideas of; Pets*)

There are several factors to consider when deciding whether to take a child to a funeral. How old is the child? How is the funeral planned? (Will the coffin be open or closed?) Will the funeral be extremely emotional? That is, will there be hysterical people, screaming and fainting? What was the child's relationship with the person who has died?

If the dead person was in the immediate family I think it is generally best to bring the child to the funeral. The experience of grief is psychologically valuable to a child who has lost someone close to him. I have known many adults who were kept away from the funeral of someone to whom they were close, and who consequently lived with vivid fantasies of that person. Because they were never allowed to participate in the funeral, they missed the opportunity that this ritual of finality provides in helping people fully accept the death of those close to them.

If a young child is to be present at a funeral, I would encourage you to arrange to have the coffin closed to minimize the trauma of seeing a dead person. If the child is under five or six, it may terrify him to be subjected to the extreme hysteria of some mourners. I do believe, however, that it is important for a child to see other people grieve over the loss of someone of whom they have been fond. It shows that other people cared about that person as well.

G

GIFTED CHILD
(SEE ALSO *Boredom*)

Several problems can come up in relation to the gifted child. In most schools, work is geared to the average child. In such an atmosphere, a gifted child can be so bored that he does not perform well academically, despite his high intelligence, talent, or creative abilities. I have known many gifted children who were labeled "troublemakers," "class clowns," and other negatives, because their boredom led them to use their gifts to make marvelous paper airplanes to fly at their classmates, or to write clever poems that mocked their teachers.

Gifted children are sometimes more anxious than other children. Their imaginations are better developed, so they are able to see more threatening or dangerous possibilities within any situation. "Where does he get such ideas?" teachers may ask, with alarm. "I don't know how he found out about such things!" parents may respond. A nuclear holocaust may be beyond the imagining of an average child, but for a gifted child, it may be a very real and frightening possibility. In a sense, the gifted child may have the mind of a twenty-year-old in the body of a ten-year-old, with a ten-year-old's emotions.

Because they are different, gifted children are sometimes ridiculed by other children, especially those who envy them. For this reason, gifted children sometimes have difficulty making friends with children their own age. Professionals can counsel parents about how to help the gifted child find intellectual stimulation without losing out emotionally.

GRANDPARENTS
(SEE ALSO *Discipline and Punishment*)

Grandparents hold a unique position in your child's life. They have had the experience of raising their own children and as they get on in years look forward to another generation of descendants. Children can gain a great deal from their relationships with their grandparents. They can feel more secure in the knowledge that there are people other than their parents who love them very much. In fact, since grandparents do not have to deal with the responsibility of actually bringing up their grandchildren, they can sometimes give them the sort of total, unconditional acceptance that parents sometimes have difficulty giving them, and indeed, that the grandparents may still have difficulty giving their own children.

This means that many children can count on their grandparents for attention and affection. If grandparents live nearby, many of them can give children solace and comfort and sanctuary when there is trouble at home. If they live far away, many can offer a visit that is an adventure and an education. Grandparents can give children a sense of history, of continuity, of belonging.

Some parents find grandparents generous to a fault. They may label them indulgent, especially if children use such manipulative ploys as, "If you won't let me have it, Grandma will."

The way to deal with this is to say, "I know Grandma and Grandpa let you do most of the things you want—even things we disapprove of—and that's all right in their house, but it is not acceptable here at home." Clearly, it is destructive to have your authority undermined by overindulgent grandparents. If the indulgences are conducted in a conspiratorial manner, such as, "Don't tell your parents about this. It will be our secret," then the problem is even more serious.

The best thing to do is to communicate openly and show respect for your parents' feelings. You can make it clear to them that you may be forced to consider restricting the children's visits. While this may be an unappealing idea—even to you—remember that effecting consistent discipline is one of your primary responsibilities as a parent.

Sometimes, grandparents whose views are opposed to yours—on political matters, for instance—may try to impress upon their grandchildren values that are inconsistent with yours. However, children's attitudes are most influenced by the people in whom they have the greatest trust and with whom they have the greatest amount of contact.

There is one other issue associated with grandparents that I would like to discuss: senility. In a family where young children and grandparents are close, it can sometimes be confusing or frightening to youngsters to observe an elderly grandparent become forgetful, moody, or otherwise behave oddly. If this happens in your family, explain that Grandma or Grandpa has become very, very old and that sometimes when people get to be this old they have trouble thinking and remembering. Explain that in some cases they even forget the names of the people they love, and sometimes do not even recognize them. Tell your children that this does not happen to everyone, but it seems that their grandparent is changing. Make it clear that all the love their grandparent had for them is still there, even if it is not expressed in the same way. You should point out to your children that they are in no way responsible for this situation. Encourage them to ask you questions and do your best to explain in a way that they will understand. Even though your children may be saddened by contact with their grandparent, they will be better prepared, with your reassurance and support, for one of life's realities. When your children show their continued love of their grandparent, be sure to express your pride in them.

GUILT
(SEE ALSO *Conscience, Discipline and Punishment*)

I believe that guilt can be a very positive force in life, insofar as it serves as a guide to reinforce behavior that is socially acceptable and helpful to other people. When people act in ways that are unkind or destructive, a healthy sense of guilt causes them to reevaluate their behavior and act in ways that are more considerate and generous in the future.

Therefore, in my opinion, there is nothing wrong with parents letting their children know when their misbehavior causes unhappiness or discomfort. Children should realize that their behavior does indeed have an effect on others. If parents do *not* show their feelings about how their children act, children will in all likelihood think that their parents don't care about them; in addition, the children will lack standards or values on which to model their own behavior.

On the other hand, it is certainly wrong for parents to attempt to control their children by playing on their emotions and arousing guilt in unfair ways. Although such extremely manipulative parents may seem to be successful, at least some of the time, in coercing their children into complying with their wishes, the children are angry—and rightfully so—about such manipulation. Children should not get the idea that they are responsible for *all* their parents' feelings. Such an idea puts an unfair burden on children and can be destructive. If parents are going through prolonged periods of anger or depression due to personal problems, they should make it clear that the children are not the cause of this upset.

It's also important to bear in mind that some children who get into trouble repeatedly may do so in order to elicit a reaction from their parents. When this occurs, parents usually have failed to give their children the positive recognition and attention they have needed in their daily lives, and probably have ignored them except when they have gotten into trouble.

In short, there's nothing wrong with letting children know when they cause you unhappiness. But you must also point out with equal vigor the joy, happiness, and pride they bring into your life with their cooperation and achievements.

H

HANDICAPPED OR CHRONICALLY ILL CHILD
(SEE ALSO *Hospitalization, Illness, Retardation, Suffering, Terminal Illness*)

The handicapped or chronically ill child needs to feel as much like other people as possible. He needs to attempt to overcome his handicap and do things. He needs his parents' encouragement, their emphasis on his strengths and abilities, rather than on what he is unable to do.

Parents should avoid being patronizing and overprotective, and constantly intervening for the handicapped or chronically ill child. Yet, they should be open and honest in recognizing his limitations. Perhaps if they see their child struggling with some problem, they can let him continue to struggle until he asks for help, rather than rushing in to say, "I'll do that for you."

It's important for all parents to provide their children with emotional stability early in life—an emotional stability that will serve the child in coping with whatever stresses occur later on. Whatever the child's resources, the parents' role is to prepare him to cope with these stresses. Because chronic illness or a handicap constitutes a stress in itself, it is especially important for a disabled child to be emotionally healthy in order to cope with that stress. One of the chief reasons the handicapped or chronically ill child's reactions to life are often different from those of other children is the parents' reactions to him. Remember, parental reactions are by far the most

93

important element in the formulation of any child's feelings about himself and the world.

If you have other children who are not handicapped you will have to explain, at some point, the problems of your handicapped child. I think you should be open and direct: explain the child's special situation as best you can and ask for your other children's help in dealing with it. Tell them you will always be available to answer questions and explain that, even though their handicapped sibling receives a great deal of attention, you are equally concerned about what is happening to them. Your attitude will not only demonstrate your acceptance of each individual family member but will help everyone deal with the problems and pressures that may arise. By teaching compassion to your children, you can help them be thankful for what they have and at the same time help them feel satisfaction and pride in offering their own resources and abilities to help others.

There may be times when your other children feel neglected. Their resentment will usually be directed more toward you than toward their handicapped sibling. The best way to handle this is to consider giving the other children undivided attention at times when they don't demand it but would certainly like to have it. The child who arouses concern only when he protests, learns to have fits of anger when he wants something. But if you recognize this need and try to provide gratification of it when everything is going well, the outbursts by the rest of your family should be offset—and your other children will be able to give greater affection to their handicapped sibling.

HEAD BANGING
(SEE ALSO *Aggression, Anger, Autism, Neurological Disturbances*)

Some children, when frustrated, will bang their heads on hard objects. Generally speaking, this is not normal. Sometimes children hurt themselves by accident when having a temper tantrum, but if time after time they continue to engage in self-destructive behavior, it is generally a sign that they are overwhelmed by aggressive tendencies that they are unable to deal with.

When children are frustrated, it is necessary for them to drain off the resultant hostility in some way. Generally their aggression is channeled outward to some object or person in their environment, but if such outlets are blocked, the child may have no choice but to direct his rage in toward himself.

It has been my experience over the years that some children who feel unimportant to their parents—and, therefore, insignificant in general—may engage in self-destructive behavior. I suggest that parents do their best to minimize the amount of frustration their child encounters and attempt to reassure and comfort him when he does become frustrated. If his head banging does not stop after these efforts, then I feel that it *may* reflect an underlying emotional problem, and would urge seeking professional help. While it may be difficult to diagnose such a disorder when a child is quite young, at least some initial consultation and periodic follow-up will help determine, as time passes, whether or not the head banging is a serious problem.

HERO WORSHIP
(SEE ALSO *Adolescence, Independence, Individuality*)

It is not at all uncommon for young people to feel intense admiration of a well-known person. Identification with such a person can help a child develop his own identity and define his own aspirations. In order for a child to establish relationships with people his own age, he must relinquish some of his ties with his parents. This transition takes place as he shifts his admiration and all-consuming interest to someone outside his home. The idealization of a hero is frequently a step toward a child's independence and individuality. Children's heroes, such as athletes or musicians, often represent ideas and characteristics that are socially beneficial and bring others satisfaction and pleasure. When children pick someone to idolize, they too want the recognition and the sense of pride and achievement that these heroes have.

Never belittle your child's desire to emulate a figure of strength or skill. However, if your child declares that he wants to be "just like" his idol, you might explain that there will never be another person exactly like his hero, while still encouraging him in his ambition to do an outstanding job. At the same time, do not encourage him to achieve something that far exceeds his ability; even as you support his efforts, help him to be realistic in evaluating his own abilities and setting his own goals. I believe that children—and adults, too, for that matter—should compete not with others, but with themselves, always striving to improve their own skills.

HOMEWORK
(SEE ALSO *Boredom, School, Teacher*)

If homework is repetitive "busy work" that simply takes time to do and provides little or no educational value, it makes sense that children are loath to complete their assignments. Uninspiring homework given in large quantities causes children to view school as an unpleasant and tedious place, and the educational process as an obstacle to self-expression. I would much prefer to see homework assignments that provide children with an opportunity to explore areas that are of particular interest to them. This would not only be more emotionally and intellectually satisfying, but would teach children how to apply the resources and tools they've learned in school to extend the horizons of their knowledge in the everyday world.

At the same time, it is not necessary that every homework assignment be a fascinating and joyful experience. Children do have to learn to complete tasks and responsibilities that are boring or tedious or lack stimulation. Explain to your child that you, too, in your work and your everyday life, have to do things that are sometimes less than scintillating—but that's life.

It may be asking too much to expect your child to enjoy doing homework, but I think you can get him to accept it. Assist your child as much as you can, but under no circumstances should you do the homework for him. Help him establish a routine for doing homework, preferably one that involves no friction with you and is compatible with his other afterschool activities.

Nagging or threatening simply puts more pressure on your child and makes things worse. Moreover, it places you in a position where you may be seen by your child as dispassionate, uncooperative, and unconcerned about his dilemma. By participating actively to help with his problem, you are showing your understanding of his feelings, demonstrating a method for tackling an unpleasant task, and preventing that overwhelming panic a child feels when there is so little time and so much homework to do.

HOMOSEXUALITY

In the psychological and psychiatric communities, homosexuality is now officially considered an "alternative lifestyle," rather than a pathology, despite the fact that some members of each community continue to believe that it is pathological. The mental health professionals' degree of acceptance of various theories concerning how and why homosexuality begins has fluctuated in recent years as well. The current thinking of the majority is that there is a biological predisposition to homosexuality that may have its basis in prenatal life. Other theories suggest that it is derived from the parent-child relationship, and still others that it is predominantly culturally determined.

Some parents are concerned about the possibility that their children may develop a homosexual lifestyle. Many homosexuals who are raising children are facing the issue of how open their lifestyle should be. In my viewpoint, where anxiety exists about homosexuality there needs to be some effort to come to terms with that anxiety, whether it be from a homosexual youth who would prefer to be heterosexual, or a parent who has a homosexual child and feels devastated by it, or by anyone else with any related concern. Dealing with the issue is in everyone's best interest. If there is intense anxiety that is somewhat incapacitating, the person who is experiencing the intense anxiety should by all means see a psychologist or a psychiatrist. If the anxiety is less than intense, I recommend that family members deal with it in the same way they deal with all family concerns—by discussing it openly. In general, the young people with whom I've talked about homosexuality seem to be much more open-minded than earlier generations. They are less inclined to judge a person on the basis of his sexual orientation.

Some parents have asked me whether they should be concerned about homosexuality if their little girl refuses to wear dresses or frilly things and prefers to play with cars and trucks rather than dolls, or if their little boy spends most of his time playing with girls rather than boys. Most children show periodic fluctuations in their interests. The girl who wears blue jeans today may wear ruffles tomorrow, and the boy who carries a doll around with him when he is small may become a fullback in years to come. In my opinion, parents should play down sex-role stereotypes to their children. The best way to do this is by example. If the mother's and father's responsibilities and interests are interchangeable enough so that the child does not make a sharp distinction between the mother role and the father role, he will not make a sharp distinction between the activities that are appropriate for males and the activities that are appropriate for females. A child's identity as a male or female will emerge spontaneously from a good, solid relationship with one or both parents.

Some parents express concern about their children being taught by homosexual schoolteachers. In my opinion, a teacher's competence should be evaluated separately from his or her private practices. Of course, if a teacher—whether homosexual or heterosexual—becomes sexually involved with a student, his professionalism and ethics should be examined and evaluated. In my experience, however, there have been many more such offenses by heterosexuals than by homosexuals.

Can a homosexual be a good parent? From a theoretical point of view, a child's emotional needs in the course of development can be met by anyone who is warm, loving, responsive, and respectful of the child's needs, regardless of that person's sexual orientation. However, what concerns me most about a parent is whether or not he can provide his child with the *optimal* conditions for the child's growth and development. For this reason, if a husband and wife have extremely demanding careers and know they are going to have little time available to raise children, I do not encourage them to become parents. In the same way, if a single person expresses the desire to have a baby without living with the baby's other parent, I do not encourage this either—even though I am convinced that many single parents who are single because of divorce or the death of their spouse have done a better job of child raising then have the combined heads of traditional two-parent families. Likewise, I have misgivings about recommending that a homosexual deliberately have a child with the intention of raising the child not with the child's other parent but with the homosexual's lover. The essential point here is that I don't think it's wise to take on the enormous commitment and responsibility of parenthood with *any* disadvantage.

Sometimes, however, a person only discovers his suppressed homosexuality after he has married and is a parent. In such cases, the parent's homosexuality should not be the single determining factor insofar as which parent receives "custody" of the child, or how much time the non-custodial parent is granted in "visitation rights." Whenever it comes to an evaluation of child custody and the associated issues, a great number of factors should be taken into consideration; the decision should not be made on just the basis of the parents' sexual orientation.

There has been a great deal of prejudice concerning homosexuals. Many people have treated homosexuality not only as a disease, but as a contagious disease. They fear that if a child has a homosexual teacher, it will cause the child to become a homosexual, or if a child is raised by a homosexual parent, the child will become homosexual. I know of no research that supports either of these notions. In fact, in the course of my many years as a psychologist I have never known a homosexual who had homosexual parents. I am inclined to think there is no direct connection between the two. I believe that a child's sexual identification is determined by a multitude of factors. I also believe that we should not judge human beings on the basis of age, gender, race, religion, nationality, or sexual orientation.

HOSPITALIZATION
(SEE ALSO *Doctor, Handicapped or Chronically Ill Child, Illness, Terminal Illness*)

I think it's very important for parents to have the opportunity to stay with a child in the hospital as much as possible, including during the night. Many hospitals now provide that opportunity; some have reclining chairs, or chairs that open into beds, for parents to sleep in overnight.

The staff in hospitals sometimes discourage long visits, complaining that children are more upset when their parents are around. I disagree. Children will express their feelings more to parents than to the hospital staff, who are less emotionally involved with them. But this doesn't mean they are less upset. For years I've been in hospitals where parents can visit freely, stay overnight, and accompany children to most procedures. I can attest to the fact that this is reassuring to the child, and serves to prevent many problems I've seen develop when parents were limited to rigid daytime visiting hours.

In preparing your child for a stay in the hospital, the important thing is to tell her the truth about what she can expect. It is perfectly understandable for a child to be anxious and apprehensive about the uncertainties and possibly painful procedures that are part of hospitalization. But the more you can eliminate the uncertainties and provide emotional support for your child during her stay, the more her anxiety will be reduced.

Give her an honest account of what will occur. Speak to the nurses as well as the doctors and ask them to keep you informed of what, when, where, and how things will be done to your child. In this way you can help prepare your child.

If you lie to your child about going in the hospital and what will happen there, she will lose trust in you and in the hospital personnel, become angry and defiant, and resist medical care. Children's distrust is very hard to correct after such an experience of being lied to or misled even once. Moreover, it makes a child a difficult patient and one whose attitude about health care can become so negative that it can influence her pattern of health care throughout life. Adults who avoid regular medical checkups or neglect important symptoms are frequently people who can trace their resentment toward the health care profession to some of their early childhood experiences with doctors and hospitals.

You can tell your child when something is going to hurt or be uncomfortable for a little while, and that you'll understand if she feels like crying. By doing this, you are honest, accepting of her feelings, and giving her encouragement to mobilize her own resources to cope with an unpleasant situation. You may find that she comes through it all without hysterics or tears. If this is the case, let her know how brave you feel she is, by explaining that you know how much it hurt—and she didn't even cry. On the other hand, if your child is upset and does cry, you can say, "Yes, I understand —it does hurt." Either way, the child has used her own abilities to deal with a situation, and has had the compassionate backup of an adult. (Even if your child is too young to understand what is happening to her, it is still possible to provide her with protection and emotional security by staying with her as much as possible. So much communication between parent and child takes place through gesture and behavior.)

Many hospitals have Child Life Programs, which enable children to visit a playroom to paint, draw, make things, or play games. Usually these are staffed with trained recreation workers who visit the children's rooms if they are unable to get to the playroom.

In most hospitals for children, the nursing staff is very sensitive to the needs of children and is generally skillful in preparing children for operations and other procedures. The most effective technique uses miniature equipment and dolls. The nurse is able to explain about the anesthesia and what the surgery will be like. Small intravenous bottles and needles are sometimes used on a doll to show the child how she may get the liquid her body needs before and after the operation. The cooperation of the child is solicited by getting her to participate with the nurse in this preoperative doll play. The result of this whole procedure is that the child becomes more familiar with what will happen so that she will be less apprehensive and ultimately less traumatized psychologically than if she knew nothing.

In helping your child prepare for surgery, stress to her that she will not be aware of the pain or feel anything during the operation because she will be asleep. If your child has not been prepared for surgery and learns later, as she surely will, that it all took place while she was asleep, and without her prior knowledge, she will likely develop some apprehension, if not a full-blown fear, of going to sleep. After all, if something was cut off or cut out while she was asleep, something similar may happen the next time she goes to sleep.

Nighttime can be particularly frightening to hospitalized children; they are in a strange setting, frequently suffering from pain, and hearing noises and sounds around them from other patients who may be in discomfort. Adding to their fright may be the fact that different people take care of their needs at night than during the day. For this reason, I encourage hospitals to allow parents to stay overnight with their children, to provide some continuity and emotional support.

Some children prefer to "go it alone" at nighttime simply to show their independence and capacity to cope. Don't hesitate to speak to your child about this, and if she feels that you needn't stay overnight with her, by all means accept her wishes.

However, I think it is sufficiently important for hospitals to allow parents to stay overnight with their children, should they desire it, that parents should make every effort to find a hospital that permits this. Parents can offer continuity of care as well as the kind of emotional support that no one else in the life of the child can potentially provide.

HYPERACTIVITY
(SEE ALSO *Neurological Disturbances*)

In my opinion, hyperactivity is related to the nervous system's inability to shut out all the unimportant stimulation, so the capacity to concentrate or focus attention cannot operate effectively. To simplify what occurs, as most people read this page about 5% of their brain is being used to concentrate; the other 95% is being used to shut out extraneous stimuli such as the sound of a truck driving down the street, the sight of curtains waving in the breeze, the smell of bread baking, the feel of a headache, and so on. If this 95% does not function well, the person will not be able to shut out all these outside things, so he will not be able to focus on reading. That's how the hyperactive child feels when he tries to read or concentrate on anything. The hyperactive child is so easily distracted that a slight tear in or spot on the page can draw his attention away from the printed words. That's also why, when tranquilizers are given to hyperactive children, they often have what is called a "paradoxical effect." That is, they make the children wilder rather than calmer, because the tranquilizer "weakens" all brain activity, thus weakening further the already ill-functioning 95% that should shut out distractions. Conversely, if we give "activating" medication to hyperactive children, it frequently calms them, thus helping them to focus better.

Because of their inability to focus, hyperactive children are constantly on the move, constantly touching things, constantly questioning things. It is difficult for most people to be with a hyperactive child without saying, "Don't do that," repeatedly. These constant negatives diminish a child's sense of self-esteem. Many times this sort of behavior is first seen as a definite problem when the child begins school, and his inability to concentrate interferes both with his learning and his socializing. In a permissive or unstructured environment, the problem is magnified. Hyperactive children do far better in a school situation that has clearly developed limits, and where instructions are clear and concrete, rather than abstract— that is, if the teachers say, "Please pick up your pencils now, read question number one, and write down your answer," rather than, "Let's get started." It is in school that hyperactive children often get labeled as troublemakers, clowns, or behavior problems. Unfortunately, these labels further diminish the children's self-esteem.

I have treated many hyperactive children. In my own practice, eleven out of twelve hyperactive children have been diagnosed as hyperactive due to neurological dysfunction. I have found that these children have benefited enormously from the carefully monitored use of medication. With medication, the children begin to gain control of themselves, which brings more positive reactions from parents, teachers, and peers; the hyperactive children thus begin to like themselves more. Parents whose children have been treated tell me, "Now I'm really enjoying being a parent. For the first time, I can sit down and play games with my child. He seems to be enjoying *himself* more."

Reputable pediatricians have reported clinical evidence that certain dietary changes can eliminate hyperactivity. Parents should consult their pediatrician to attempt to find an experienced pediatric allergist who can track down those foods that might lead to hyperactivity.

Most hyperactive children are boys. It's not certain why, but one possibility is the influence of hormonal factors, because a great deal of hyperactivity diminishes in puberty. Some people react to a hyperactive child by saying, "Boys will be boys," "Or he's just an active kid—he'll grow out of it." Others look for an emotional problem: "He's upset because his grandmother died" or "He's reacting to his parents' divorce." I believe that the moment you begin to think your child might be hyperactive, you should have him evaluated by an experienced, licensed pediatric neurologist and a clinical child psychologist. With the help of a detailed developmental history—including a history of the pregnancy, birth, and immediate postpartum period—in conjunction with a neurological examination and specific psychological tests, in all likelihood a treatment plan can be worked out for your child. Your pediatrician can refer you to a pediatric neurologist and a clinical child psychologist.

Not all cases of hyperactivity are due to neurological dysfunction. In some instances, it's a symptom related to anxiety and has more of an emotional than a physiological cause. Also, in children with hypoglycemia there are symptoms of irritability and difficulty in focusing when the blood sugar level is low. In any event, the kind of evaluation I have suggested will serve to determine the basis for your child's symptoms and the appropriate recommendations can be made.

I

ILLNESS
(SEE ALSO *Doctor, Handicapped or Chronically Ill Child, Hospitalization, Medication, Terminal Illness*)

When children become ill they are understandably anxious, as are their parents. This anxiety causes parents and health professionals to be more vigilant and to give more attention to the child than she would normally receive. Not only is this a sensible response, it is also very appropriate to the child's physical and mental health. Even if a child is too young to understand her illness, the emotional comfort that is communicated by a concerned and sympathetic parent will contribute greatly to a child's recovery.

Some parents, who are very protective of their children, tend to overreact sometimes to a child's physical complaints. This overreaction can cause some children to feign illness in order to gain attention or avoid unpleasant situations. I believe that, initially, it is best for parents to take a somewhat matter-of-fact attitude and not react in an extreme way when a child complains of symptoms. As a general rule I suggest you take your child's temperature. If she doesn't have a fever, but just complains of "feeling weird" or having a headache or a stomachache, you should send her off to school. It's true that it is a calculated risk to send a child with physical complaints to school, but you have to weigh this against the effects that such a pattern of behavior can have on a child in the long run.

When a child uses illness as an excuse to avoid some unpleasantness, I think you should let her know that you understand why she feels as she does and at the same time express confidence that she will get through it all right and will feel better as soon as she is involved in the experience. Such emotional support will help your child master her uneasy feelings and develop greater strength that she can recall the next time she feels insecure in a situation. The main thing is that you not reward illness in a way that encourages your child to use it for getting out of tasks she would rather avoid.

If your child complains frequently about aches and pains, you should without a doubt take her to a physician. You should also try to find out whether your child is under stress or why she may be feeling some anxiety. In my experience I have found that children often report feeling bad when exams are coming up or the workload in school is too heavy. Sometimes an overbearing teacher or school bully is making a child's life difficult.

I advise against letting children watch television during the hours they would otherwise be in school; it's better for them to rest and sleep instead. If your child seems able to engage in some activity, have her do schoolwork. You can contact the school and find out what her assignments are.

Children sometimes have difficulty coping with parental illness. As I have said, they see parents as omnipotent—in their minds you do heroic things and take away discomfort. So when a parent falls ill, it can be upsetting to a child. I think this situation can be approached matter-of-factly by telling your children that you don't feel well and need some help until you feel better. Remind them that when they have been ill, it felt good to have someone take care of them and do little things that made it easier until they were healthy again.

If a parent is suffering from a chronic illness, or has had a heart attack, it's important to let the children know that father, for example, may have to be less active and may not be able to do some of the things he was able to do before. Nevertheless, it's important to point out that in no way will it affect his love for them. I advise against trying to hide parental illness from children; they are usually too perceptive for this kind of deception. Sickness is a very real part of life and hiding makes it more frightening than it need be.

IMAGINARY COMPANIONS

The presence of a make-believe playmate is not unusual in the life of a child, and is not emotionally harmful as long as your child is aware that it is make-believe, and that you know this too. It is important for children to be able to make the distinction between what is real and what is imaginary. Some parents are afraid that they will rob a child of the pleasure of play by making this clear, but their fears are unfounded. Children can relate quite vividly and emotionally to make-believe events, and this gives them great latitude for the expression of their ideas and feelings.

Children sometimes try to resolve the real problems of their lives through their play. For instance, they may attribute their own misbehavior to an imagined companion, thus engaging in unacceptable activities and at the same time living a life free of guilt. Needless to say, it's unwise to allow children to absolve themselves of their misdeeds without some feelings of remorse, or some punishment. You should let your child know that she is the one responsible for all the things that her imaginary playmate does and that she will have to pay the consequences of the playmate's wrongdoing. If such a situation is handled in this way, I predict that the imaginary mischief-maker will shape up—or else your child will send her companion on its way as easily as she conjured it up in the first place.

INCEST
(SEE ALSO *Oedipus Complex*)

Incest is a complex problem, and by no means a rare event. It occurs between fathers and daughters perhaps more frequently than between mothers and sons. Brothers and sisters have also been known to have sexual relationships with one another.

A child bears a tremendous burden when incest occurs. Often she is fearful of discontinuing it, and fearful of confessing to it. She may want to avoid the incestuous parent's wrath; or she may want to avoid causing the incestuous parent to be punished. The child who is a victim of incest in many cases feels responsible, as if she had caused it to occur, even though in fact she may not have initiated it. This is one reason why the child is frequently protective of the incestuous parent. I worked with an adolescent girl who was having intercourse with her paternal grandfather. For years, the girl had been afraid to tell anyone. She was afraid of being responsible for the grandfather's criminal prosecution. She was also afraid of being the cause of the destruction of the father/grandfather relationship. In addition to such fears, there is always the additional possibility that the child derives some pleasure from the incestuous relationship, despite the anguish it involves; this pleasure only intensifies the child's guilt. Understandably, the effect of incest on a child's later sexual adjustment is very profound, and it is extremely difficult to repair the damage.

Even indirect sexual experience—as when a parent behaves seductively toward a child—can be damaging. The child who is encouraged in, and thus unable to give up a strong attachment to the parent of the opposite sex may feel guilty about relating sexually to *any* member of the opposite sex.

One note of caution: As important as it is to be sensitive to this issue, it's also important to avoid making an accusation unless there's fairly clear evidence. Recently I was involved in the case of a mother who, having lost custody of her daughter to the father, vindictively accused the father of sexually abusing the child. By law, this accusation required an investigation. The child was separated from her father and temporarily placed in a foster home. She was interrogated by numerous professional and legal authorities. This situation created intense anxiety in the child, put her in the position of feeling she had caused her separation from her father, and damaged the mother-child relationship.

INDEPENDENCE
(SEE ALSO *Adolescence, Allowance, Dating, Defiance, Fears, Friends, Hero Worship, Individuality, Infancy, Juvenile Delinquency, Listening, Model Child, Rebellion*)

Toward the middle of the first year of life, a baby will begin to show an increased desire to do things by himself. He will find it satisfying to move around in his environment and manipulate objects.

In order to become more independent, a baby needs to develop certain skills. Basically, he can only become independent if his dependent needs have been met. Many parents believe that they will "spoil" their infant and keep him in a "babyish" state if they meet his needs for cuddling and stimulation. The reverse is true. If a baby's needs are met, he will become *more* independent and self-sufficient than if his needs are ignored and he is allowed to "cry it out," or is otherwise pushed toward independence before he is ready. Simply, when needs are met, they subside; when needs are frustrated, they persist. If early dependency needs are not met, the child clings to infantile behavior patterns and even carries them into adult life. If early dependency needs are met, the child is able to develop and use his own resources, so that eventually he has the skills for coping independently as an adult.

Just as parents' not responding to their infant's needs will interfere with the baby's independence, parents who prevent their older children from using the abilities they have will also interfere with the development of independence. Some parents may do this by pointing out to their children every possible hazard that might befall them from the moment they get out into the world. I've known of parents who have frightened their children into clinging to them by overwhelming them with more do's and don't's than they needed.

One major transition toward greater independence takes place when a child begins school. Probably the most useful way for a parent to react to this is matter-of-factly, honestly appraising the situation and expressing confidence in the child's ability to handle school. Your constant reassurances that there is nothing to worry about can only prepare your child for failure. If there is nothing to worry about, why are you carrying on so? It's much better to tell him, on the first day of school, that most children feel a little sad at times like this, but that they get over it and you know he will too.

Whether he worries or not will be determined less by your telling him not to worry than by his seeing that you aren't worried yourself. I can't stress enough that a parent's confidence in a child's ability is a very important factor in the child's independence.

Probably among the first signs that a school child is becoming independent is when he begins to separate himself from home and family, spending more of his time with children his age. Throughout childhood and adolescence, children find emotional support for the journey from home in each other's company. They belong to their own groups and secret clubs, have their own codes and rituals, games, chants, and jokes. All of these activities emphasize their separation from adults and solidarity with each other. But in order for a child to become truly independent of his parents, he must have acquired trust in his parents and confidence in himself early in life. Otherwise, he will still be struggling between dependence and independence.

It is most important that parents be able to accept, emotionally as well as intellectually, the increasing independence of the child and his capacity to engage in a world outside of their influence. In some sense, many parents would like to keep their child close beside them, to enjoy their child as an extension of themselves. However, if they want their child to become an adult, they must accept and find gratification in their child's efforts to do things for himself.

If the challenge of parenthood can be reduced to one basic task, it is the task of helping children develop their own talents, skills, and resources for coping with life *without* their parents.

For this reason, I sometimes feel more comfortable with and appreciative of children who are challenging, and even moderately defiant on occasion, children who express some willfulness and assertiveness, rather than those who are withdrawn, compliant, goody-goody "model" children.

Unfortunately many parents focus a great deal of attention on teaching children to obey, rather than to think for themselves. Many schools reward compliance and docility, and are punitive toward children who even question authority. Most young adults I've known who have gotten into difficulty have done so not because they were purposefully defiant, but because they did not know how to deal with freedom. These children were initially so obedient and repressed that when they were given some degree of freedom they simply let loose and did not know how to stop themselves. Children who know how to deal with freedom do not need a parent or a teacher or a leader telling them exactly what to do and how and when to do it. They have learned *self*-control.

A parent can begin teaching a child to develop his own internal controls by teaching him to make independent choices. Even a very young child can make independent but guided choices. A toddler who likes to hear a bedtime story can be given a choice of two or three books. When he is dressing, he can be asked, "Would you prefer to wear your blue overalls or your green?" At the playground, he can be consulted: "Would you like to go down the slide first or on the swings?"

In this way, a parent teaches a child that he is capable of making choices, that his wishes and feelings are respected, that he can participate in his own fate. Such a child will not be submissive in adult life. He won't need to look for someone to tell him what to do.

People who join cults or surrogate families are generally seeking to belong to a group that gives them a sense of self-esteem, recognition, and importance. When young people have these needs satisfied by their own families they are far less likely to seek out other groups.

People who join a cult are trading their freedom for what they perceive as protection. As many of us recall, the members of the Guyana People's Temple were so unable to deal with their own freedom that in exchange for the "protection" of their leader, Jim Jones, they agreed to a suicide pact and ultimately committed mass suicide.

I would venture to say that if these people had been taught how to deal with their freedom, how to make their own choices, if they had gained a sense of individuality and self-respect, they would have been far less likely to join the cult, and certainly less likely to follow the murderous orders of a maniacal leader.

It is not always easy for a parent to allow a child choices, to demonstrate that the child's wishes and feelings are respected, to grant the child some participation in his own fate. Nor is it always easy for a child to make his own decisions and live with the consequences. It would be much simpler, in a sense, for a parent to adopt one set of rules and regulations, stick with them, and enforce compliance with them in the child. But if a parent is to help a child not only grow up physically, but become truly adult, the parent needs to prepare the child to live independently of the parent, to think for himself, to make his own decisions, and live with the consequences. There is no other way for a child to become an adult. And there is not a more challenging task for parent *or* child.

INDIVIDUALITY
(SEE ALSO *Adolescence, Dating, Defiance, Hero Worship, Independence, Juvenile Delinquency, Listening, Rebellion*)

It is crucially important for parents to accept their child's individuality. I can well understand any parent wishing to share his or her own interests with a child, and I can also understand some disappointment if a child takes on interests that are completely different from those of a parent. Likewise, I realize that it may not always be easy for a parent to understand a child whose temperament differs markedly from his or her own. Nevertheless, it is essential that parents do everything they can to accept their child's individuality, praise and encourage their child in whatever she does best, and create a relationship with her that is based upon her uniqueness.

If a child is not accepted, if she cannot live up to her parents' expectations, and cannot gain a feeling of being important to her parents without losing her own individuality, she may become very rebellious in an effort to establish her independence. Or, her self-esteem may diminish; she may come to feel defeated by life and may possibly cope with pressure by lowering her levels of aspiration, thus avoiding the anxiety caused by any demands that tax her abilities, for fear that she may not "measure up."

In our culture, adolescence is a stage during which one can predict with near certainty that a child will reject her parents' ideas and turn to opposing ones. This is nothing to worry about. It's part of the normal pattern through which we all establish our own identity, individuality, and self-esteem. In their search for their identity, most teenagers try out things that their parents consider unacceptable. Many teenagers simply sample things once in order to feel they've experienced them, and then stop. Obviously, young people need to have some protection from dangers that can lead to irreversible tragedies, but for the most part it's important for parents to help their teenagers develop the resources for being able to cope with life's problems later on. Parents can do this by respecting their child's individuality. Not only is it difficult—and sometimes impossible—for parents to police their teenager all the time, but this is not even desirable. A child needs freedom to learn, and one often learns by making mistakes.

I do want to make it clear that parents should certainly make their teenager aware of their reactions to the teenager's behavior. But expressing opinions and feelings is one thing, and insisting on their acceptance is another. Parents should keep in mind that it is not uncommon for a teenager to ignore her parents' warnings and even do the opposite of what parents say from time to time. When your adolescent does something of which you disapprove, by all means let her know how you feel; also let her know that you realize there is basically no way you can stop her, but that you want her to know you love her a great deal and are deeply concerned about her welfare. If you have had a close and trusting relationship with her in the past, in all likelihood she will be concerned about your reactions to her behavior. Despite the teenager's defiance and rebelliousness, most want parental acceptance and love. If you accept her individuality, even while recognizing the hazards that are involved in giving her the freedom she needs, there is less chance she will defy you in self-destructive ways.

While adolescents are intent upon becoming independent of their parents, they are often equally intent upon conforming closely to the ways of their peers. If you look back on your own youth, you may remember that you "had" to have the latest Frank Sinatra or Elvis Presley or Beatles record or you would be "the only one in the world" without it, and would "absolutely die of embarrassment." Parents need to be compassionate when their child expresses her intense feelings about the realities of her life. That doesn't mean, though, that parents should allow their child's peer group to run the parents' lives or their homes. If you feel strongly that you do not want your thirteen-year-old daughter to wear high-heeled shoes, you can tell your daughter that while you respect her wishes and understand her feelings, this happens to be one issue about which you feel strongly.

If you have maintained warm and open communication with your daughter, have shown respect for her ideas and values—whether or not they correspond with your own—and have let her know your own feelings in an uncritical and low-key way, she should be able to live with her dissatisfaction on that particular issue.

INFANCY
(SEE ALSO *Breastfeeding, Curiosity, Dropping Things, Learning, Play, Prematurity, Sucking, Teething, Thumbsucking, Weaning*)

There is no such thing as a "typical" infant. Even in a nursery of newborns, some babies are fat, and some wiry, some are placid and others restless, some are vocal, some are quiet. No two are exactly alike. Each baby starts off with inherited characteristics from his parents and their ancestors; he is also influenced by his mother's condition during pregnancy; the birth itself; and the way he is treated after birth. Each baby is unique, an individual. There has never before been anyone exactly like him, and there never will be. No baby will ever have exactly that shade of red hair, combined with exactly those long limbs, exactly that lusty cry, exactly that tendency to be active and easily irritated. Each baby even has his own pattern of sucking that is almost as distinctive as his fingerprints.

But all newborn babies, a growing body of research tells us, are far more active, responsive, and complex than we used to believe. The newborn baby can see, hear, distinguish smells and tastes, and respond to touch and movement. On the very day he is born a baby can look attentively at things and can distinguish forms; within the next couple of days he can fix his gaze on an object within his field of vision and follow it with his eyes if it is gradually moved. A newborn baby can distinguish patterns; he will spend longer periods of time looking at more complex patterns, such as an outline of the human face, than he will at a similar but simpler one. The newborn can distinguish differences in pitch. He can turn his head toward the source of a sound. He can feel changes in temperature, especially around his mouth. He can distinguish tastes, and is already beginning to prefer sweet ones. He is beginning to distinguish smells, and is very sensitive to touch and pressure.

From the time a baby draws his first breath—and perhaps even before that—he is learning. At first, in the early reflex stage of development, he learns through practice in coordinating his simple motor actions with what his senses tell him about the outside world. The more opportunities he is given to look, listen, smell, taste, and touch different kinds of things, the more he learns. A baby is best able to respond to new sights and sounds when he is awake and comfortable, after he has been fed, burped, and diapered. This is his natural play time, and for the early years of his life play and learning are inseparable. If an infant has to use all his energy to cope with strong feelings of distress from within, he can't pay attention to what's going on outside him. Research has shown that newborns can focus their attention on a particular new thing, and that as a baby explores his environment he increases the number of things that interest him.

Parents help their newborn learn in ways that are natural. They talk to their baby and sing to him; they hang mobiles, tack up pictures, place toys in the crib. They rock their baby, carry him, talk to him, play with him, smile at him. Studies have shown that infants who are held, rocked, carried, talked to, played with, and smiled at are less irritable, have longer periods of concentration, develop a wider range of different responses and relate better to others. Early stimulation seems to foster greater learning.

What this means to parents is that in addition to the baby's needs for food and love, he needs other kinds of nourishment as well. He needs stimulation to grow on just as much as he needs vitamins and minerals, warmth and tenderness. It makes no more sense to say of a crying baby, "He just wants attention," than it does to say, "He just wants food." Both are real needs. Parents need to provide their newborn with an environment that will help him to develop. It is not always possible to predict the particular stresses he will meet in the course of his life, but parents can help him develop the strength and flexibility that come from a feeling of inner security, the ability to form warm relationships with other human beings, and the capacity to deal with increased stimulation or stress when it becomes necessary.

INSTINCTS
(SEE ALSO *Sucking*)

For the most part modern psychology doesn't recognize the concept of instincts. Instead, it recognizes needs or learned needs. Most psychologists feel that behavior patterns are all learned through experience. While I respect my colleagues, their theories, and experiments, I cannot disregard some of my own observations over my many years as a practicing psychologist.

Clearly there are inborn tendencies to behave in a given way. Newborn babies have what is called a "rooting" reflex, or "rooting" response, which serves to cause a baby to move in the direction of her mother's breast and begin sucking automatically. This can hardly be called a learned response, since it is present immediately after birth.

In addition, it is unquestionable that parents have strong protective feelings toward their babies. I consider this to be an inborn tendency. Mothers and fathers become anxious when a baby cries, and there is a strong tendency to pick the baby up and hold it close. This protective tendency leads a parent to find out which of the babies needs are unmet, and to attempt to gratify those needs. If the crying baby is hungry, the parents feed him; if the baby is in physical discomfort, the parents act to remove the source of discomfort.

In a sense there is a meshing of inborn tendencies that have a beautiful and natural quality. A baby sucking at its mother's breast, after satisfying its sucking needs and need for food, will generally become limp, relaxed, and will retract the facial muscles in a way that breaks the suction and has the quality of a smile. This satisfied state and the resultant smile (tightening of the facial muscles) invariably causes the mother to smile at the baby. This mutual contentment—the baby's satisfaction and relief and the mother's reduction of discomfort, plus the sensual satisfaction that comes with the baby sucking at her nipples, leads to mutual happiness, satisfaction, and a positive mother-child relationship.

While traditional psychologists might see this as a series of learned responses, I feel they are inborn tendencies that should be recognized and respected. They have important survival value for human beings.

INTELLIGENCE QUOTIENT
(SEE ALSO *Gifted Child, Learning, Retardation, School*)

An Intelligence Quotient ("I.Q.") is a number that represents a child's mental age in relation to his chronological age, as measured by the child's performance on a test compared to the performances of a cross-section of children his age.

As controversial as this may sound, intelligence tests don't necessarily reflect a child's true intelligence. I recall testing an extremely bright seven-year-old boy. When asked to explain the difference between an "optimist" and a "pessimist," he said, after much thought, "I think I got it. An optimist is an eye doctor, and a pessimist is a foot doctor!" While his answer was not correct, he displayed a creative and clever problem-solving ability. This highlights the fact that I.Q. tests are not always a valid indicator of a child's intellectual ability. The tests are indeed helpful, but they must be interpreted along with such factors as cultural background, family and other environmental experiences, and mood at the time of the test.

Clearly, people are born with a potential intelligence, but it takes environmental stimulation and enriched life experiences to help a person achieve that potential. Psychologists have never fully agreed on a definition of what intelligence is, but have at times simply said that it is what an I.Q. test measures, and let it go at that. I believe that our focus should be on helping children develop the ability to deal with life's problems as effectively as they can in a way that enables them to form positive relationships with others and to engage in socially useful activities.

L

LANGUAGE DEVELOPMENT PROBLEMS
(SEE ALSO *Baby Talk, Neurological Disturbances, Stuttering*)

It's common for parents to compare their children to other children. "Lisa began speaking in full sentences at eighteen months!" This is sometimes enough to make other parents worry about why their twenty-four-month-old is not doing the same. As with all milestones in a child's growth and development, speech and language acquisition is a highly individual matter. Most children do begin saying a few words by age fifteen months, and by the time they are two years old may be able to say 50 to 200 words. But every child develops at a different rate. As I've mentioned before, my son Eric was slow to put words together, but once he did, they became long, complicated paragraphs.

However, if a child is more than two and a half years old and has said very little, or speaks very poorly, there may be cause for concern, and you should see your pediatrician about this. Frequently, the problem is that the child is simply slow in learning muscle control, or that she has not had enough language stimulation. But a pediatrician will check, too, for other possibilities—a hearing deficiency, nerve damage that prevents the tongue from moving properly, an abnormality of the mouth. He will also look for signs of mental retardation or emotional disturbance.

If in fact the child is normal, her speech will most likely improve rapidly if her parents take care to talk and read to her often, and to name objects as they hand them to her. Often, if a child is placed in a situation with other children who already talk, this can be just the extra stimulation needed.

In any event, it is important to recognize that there is not a rigidly set standard for speech development, and that your child's developing in a different way than the child next door does not necessarily mean that there is any serious disorder.

LAZINESS
(SEE ALSO *Allowance, Boredom, Depression, Responsibility*)

There are many so-called "Super-Parents" who feel that every moment of a child's day has to be accounted for with lessons or some other programmed activity. This can be detrimental to a child. Every child should have some time of her own, even if she wants to "waste" it. You are not a neglectful parent if you don't program every moment of your child's day. In fact, the contrary is true. In my experience, children who get bored easily and say, "There's nothing to do," are children who have been programmed so much of the time that when the program is relaxed they can't function on their own.

Generally, children are active—they want to do things, they want to participate. More parents complain that they can't keep their children out of things than that they can't get their children to do things. However, sometimes children are reluctant to do things that they are asked to do because they are criticized when they do not perform to their parents' satisfaction, or because they do not receive enough parental recognition. This can also happen when a child is paid for doing household chores. Soon he reasons, "Why should I do anything unless I get paid for it?"

There are also specific stages of a child's life when she may be relatively inactive, complain of fatigue, or even sleep during the day. Usually there is a physical reason behind this. During the adolescent growth spurt, for instance, males in particular may be growing so rapidly that they need to consume large amounts of food and still rest. Some children may be tired after a hard day at school, perhaps because of lowered blood sugar. What may seem to be laziness may also mask depression. Or a child may be depressed in reaction to his parents' divorce or his grandfather's death, for example, and can leave his homework undone as a result.

What is important here is that parents avoid labeling their child as "lazy," and instead try to find out why the child is behaving in this way, and how to help him behave in ways that are more fulfilling.

LEARNING
(SEE ALSO *Boredom, Curiosity, Gifted Child, Hyperactivity, Infant, Intelligence Quotient, Play, Retardation, School, Teacher*)

From birth, children are capable of learning. In the beginning, they learn just simple lessons, but studies show quite conclusively that a child's education starts when he comes into the world. Because the newborn baby is so sensitive to his environment, he can record and incorporate experiences. For example, if you connect his foot to a mobile he will learn to make it dance by moving his foot. If you then connect the mobile to his other foot he will move that one instead. Fairly quickly, the child's body of knowledge builds. This illustrates how important his early experiences are.

I believe you can and should help your child learn from birth onward. At first this means providing a stimulating and varied environment to increase his capacity for learning. As I explain elsewhere, the baby needs things to see, hear, smell, touch, and taste.

When your child begins to learn in another way—by talking and asking questions—he may seem to be trying to exasperate you by asking the same things over and over. He will seem delighted to hear you give the same response time and time again. I know this can be taxing at times, but I can assure you that the child whose questions are answered develops an insatiable curiosity about the world.

I don't advocate pushing a child into learning. Some parents put pictures with words in big letters all over the house in an effort to teach their children to recognize the words. I don't think such parents are helping their child by playing the role of a formal teacher. Parents who force children to learn are simply satisfying their own need to show how smart their children are.

LEFT-HANDEDNESS

There is nothing wrong with being left-handed. Approximately six to eight percent of school-age children write with their left hand. Most children don't show a clear preference for one hand until they are at least two years old, and some do not reveal a preference until they are four or five. If a left-handed child is forced to use his right hand it may cause extensive psychological damage. Handedness to some degree denotes which side of the brain is dominant. Each side of the brain, as we understand it, handles different functions, but communication does take place between the two hemispheres. Sometimes when one side is damaged, the other side takes over. Parents should keep in mind when their left-handed children are learning new skills, that basically we all live in a right-handed world, and left-handed people have greater difficulty with doorknobs, scissors, and many other items that are made for right-handed use. However, for what it's worth, this author writes with his right hand and throws a ball with his left hand. He also holds a tennis racquet with his right hand, which makes throwing a ball with his left hand a great convenience.

LISTENING
(SEE ALSO *Acceptance, Adolescence, Day Care, Family, Independence, Individuality, Television*)

With technological advances such as recording devices that people can listen to by themselves, as well as TV sets that involve one-way communication, we seem to have lost something in the art of communication and in listening to human beings in person. It's not only important for parents to be patient enough to listen to children, it's important for parents to listen to each other. Many marital problems and family disturbances I've dealt with professionally have resulted from people's neglect in listening to each other's thoughts, ideas, and feelings. One of the major complaints I get from children is that "Nobody listens to me—not my parents, not my teachers, nobody. What's the use of asking questions or saying things if they're not going to listen anyway?" Such a state of affairs is demeaning for a child, and diminishes his self-esteem. Children need to be listened to as evidence of their parents' respect, acceptance, and support. If parents do not listen, some children may give up trying to communicate; some may become defiant or rebellious in order to arouse parental concern. The more you listen to your child's ideas and values—even those with which you don't agree—the more likely it is that your child will listen respectfully to the ideas and values of others, including your own.

LOVE
(SEE ALSO *Acceptance, Affection, Love-Hate Relationships, Sexual Experiences*)

I don't think I need to instruct parents on how to love their children or the importance of this feeling for the emotional health of all human beings. I will say, however, that your children are most likely to feel loved when they feel they hold an important place in your life, and when you are responsive to their needs. Children can sense when someone is distant or indifferent. If a parent is consistently indifferent, nothing will more clearly demonstrate a lack of love. It is indifference, and not hate, as many believe, that is the opposite of love.

Love is not only hard to define, but it is also a word that is used loosely. Love is perhaps best described as a feeling of being wanted and accepted unconditionally. It's a feeling you have when you hold an important place in someone's life. Feeling loved is an absolute necessity for a child in order to have the energy and motivation to grow, learn, develop, and love other people. There is no adequate substitute for love, and it is essential that parents feel and communicate love to their children, not only verbally, but through their respect and concern for, and acceptance of their children. There is no way you can verbally convince a child you love him, without showing it in your actions and behavior as well.

LOVE-HATE RELATIONSHIPS
(SEE ALSO *Arguments Between Parents, Sibling*)

Every once in a while parents will ask me what it means if their otherwise loving child occasionally becomes angry with them and screams, "I hate you!" Parents want to know if this means that their child does not love them. My answer is to ask parents whether they ever get angry with their child. Of course, all parents do at one time or another. But does this momentary, occasional anger diminish their love for their child? No. It is the same when a child becomes angry with her parents. No person loves another person all the time, no matter how deep a loving bond there is. It is perfectly natural that there are times when one person is frustrated in the relationship, and this frustration leads to anger. Actually, there is probably more anger involved in deep, loving relationships than there is in casual relationships. Anger and love are intense emotions. Therefore, any close relationship—whether it be between spouses, parents and children, or siblings—is bound to have its intense "downs" as well as "ups."

I think it is important that your child be able to express her anger to you without feeling that to do so would mean the loss of your love. If she does not express her negative emotions, they will become pent-up and cause her pressure, and it is possible that they will eventually explode in a destructive way. At the same time, I believe that children should be encouraged to express these negative feelings in ways that do not hurt or destroy the integrity of others. As a rule, children should be encouraged to express their feelings verbally, rather than in destroying objects or in lashing out physically. It is essential for children to learn to come to terms with angry feelings in a way that allows for the release of these feelings in a socially acceptable way, and the best place for this to happen is the home, in the security of a loving relationship between you and your children.

LYING
(SEE ALSO *Bragging, Cheating, Juvenile Delinquency, Stealing*)

There are a couple of ways in which parents can sometimes unwittingly contribute to their child's lying. One way is for parents themselves to tell "little white lies." An eleven-year-old girl wrote to me with this problem: One day, while her family was eating dinner, her mother gave her a lecture about lying. Then the telephone rang, and the mother answered it. The call was for the father, who was at the table, but the mother told the caller that he wasn't there. "To me," the eleven-year-old girl wrote me, "that was a big lie. Was it a lie to you?"

Yes, it certainly was. This kind of double standard—parents demanding that their child always tell the truth, but justifying their own lies—can be troublesome to a child, and can give a child a valid reason for losing faith and trust in parents. Even though the mother's motivation was to give her husband an opportunity to enjoy a pleasant, uninterrupted meal, she still told a lie. Perhaps it would have been better for her to tell the other person that her husband was "not available to talk at the moment" but could return the call later. In this way, she would have told the truth, given the father the consideration and protection she wanted to, and avoided getting caught up in a double standard.

Another way in which parents can unwittingly contribute to a child's lying is by forcing severe, strict confrontations concerning the truth, which result in punishment for admitting the truth. To illustrate this point, I recall a mother who came to me intensely angry with her sixteen-year-old daughter, convinced that the daughter was a pathological liar. This mother described opening her daughter's bedroom door to find herself enveloped in a cloud of cigarette smoke. She then asked her daughter point-blank, and in a very angry tone: "Were you smoking?" The daughter, terrified, said, "No." On the basis of this confrontation, the mother consulted me about her daughter's lying.

I asked the mother if she had experimented with cigarette smoking when she was a teenager. The mother replied that she had. I asked the mother if she had told her own mother the truth about this. The woman replied that she hadn't. "Do you consider yourself a liar?" I asked the woman. Of course, she answered that she did not. Clearly, the daughter was fearful of her mother's wrath, and defended herself by lying. I suggested to the mother that she could have avoided her daughter's lying by saying initially, "I see that you've been smoking, and I disapprove of it heartily." In this way, she would be dealing with the situation without forcing her daughter to defend herself by telling a lie.

There is another category of lying, however, and that is the chronic lying which—like chronic stealing—can be related to serious underlying emotional difficulties. This sort of lying comes about when youngsters do not develop a strong conscience or an internalized sense of right and wrong—they simply lie and steal without shame or guilt or remorse because they do not feel that they are doing wrong. This problem is very difficult to overcome if the child is much older than five and has not developed these values through a strong, loving relationship with at least one parent.

Some other children who lie while realizing that lying is wrong may continue to do so in order to retaliate against authority—authorities like parents, for whom these children have very angry feelings.

As far as punishment for lying and stealing, I believe that parents should avoid being extremely punitive. Milder forms of punishment are more effective in helping a child develop a conscience about such behavior. But whatever punishment is decided on, it's important for parents to make it clear to their child that lying is totally unacceptable behavior.

M

MASTURBATION
(SEE ALSO *Adolescence, Sex Education, Sexual Experiences*)

Masturbation—stimulation of the genitals—is not harmful. It is quite common among children, and many adults continue to masturbate. Even infants may achieve pleasure by touching their genitals. By the age of four many children have begun to masturbate. They may straddle an object and slide up and down, or place a soft object between their thighs. Stimulating their genitals around bedtime or when they are preoccupied with listening to a story or watching TV is not unusual. Children go through stages when they engage in more masturbatory activity than they do at other times—it usually decreases when children are between the ages of seven and twelve, and increases during adolescence.

I think you should take a casual, matter-of-fact approach, indicating that you understand the child's impulse to do this. Generally, children will not masturbate excessively unless there is a significant emotional problem or they are living in a somewhat unstimulating environment. Some children engage in more masturbatory activity if the parents are overly strict and force them, as a form of punishment, to be alone in their rooms without anything to do.

If your child is masturbating a great deal of the time, don't take a punitive attitude or try to instill feelings of guilt or threaten your child's self-esteem. Although some people disagree, I think it is a mistake to ignore excessive masturbation. Your child may feel more anxious if you do not react. He may engage in masturbation excessively with the secret hope that someone will set limits. Similarly, if your child masturbates in public I think you should react and say something like, "If this is what you want to do, do it when you are alone and not when there are others around." Again, don't be harsh in your attitude. Try to communicate the fact that there is nothing wrong with the child's touching himself in this way, but it is not something that other people care to watch.

Often, children explore each other's genitals. This is not unusual and represents an almost universal curiosity that is satisfied by playing, "I'll show you mine if you show me yours." I don't think a parent should overreact to this game by expressing strong disapproval or by punishing the child. Overreactions may intensify the child's feelings about sexual exploration, and that intensity may lead to increased sexual activity or even to the suppression of healthy sexual desires.

If your child and his friends engage in such games, I don't think you should ignore the activity. What you can do, in an offhand way, is let your children know that you've seen them playing this game. Suggest to them that they play something else. By giving their sexual game a mildly negative reaction, you can make clear that bottoms and genitals are not to be examined casually. You will also impart the idea that sexual stimulation and pleasure have a special significance. But don't be surprised if, in spite of your urging, this game happens again—it's perfectly understandable for a child to be fascinated by his or her own body and the bodies of others.

MEDICATION
(SEE ALSO *Doctor/Medical Examination, Hospitalization, Illness*)

Sometimes children resist taking medication because it tastes unpleasant or is uncomfortable, especially if the medicine is in the form of eyedrops, eardrops, or a suppository. If your child is old enough to understand, you need to explain to him that this is something the doctor wants him to take to help him get well. I advise you *not* to say, "Do it for your mother (or father)—it will make me so happy." This implies that he may be rejected if he doesn't. An approach like this can have detrimental psychological effects. For instance, you may find that your child then takes medicine for emotional satisfaction. If he feels unloved or unwanted, or if he has been taught to get his parents to cajole him into taking medicine in exchange for their love, he may do just that—use supposed illness to get your support.

Similarly, if you offer a reward or a toy for taking his medicine, he will get the idea that he should be rewarded with some gift for every unpleasant situation. It is far better for your child to learn to cope with these situations and discover the sense of strength that follows being able to do something difficult or distasteful.

It's understandable for a parent to feel awful about making his or her child do something unpleasant, especially if the youngster is an infant who cannot understand what is happening to him. I suggest you give the medicine as quickly and as painlessly as possible, and then offer comfort immediately afterward.

If an older child refuses to take medicine, you should make some attempt to reason with him. Be sure to acknowledge that you accept his feelings, and make things as easy for him as you can. Don't hesitate to offer candy, syrup, or anything else that may help disguise the taste. In the end, though, let your child know that he must take the medicine, and that's the way the world is; no one always has all things the way he wants them. Don't try to embarrass your child into taking the medication or make him feel that he is a baby because he is uncooperative. You will always have more luck if you accept his feelings.

MESSINESS
(SEE ALSO *Adolescence, Babysitter, Independence, Toilet Training*)

In general, I think that after your child is around six years old you needn't feel compelled to pick up after him. At this age he can take on the responsibility of putting his dirty clothes in the hamper and making his bed. Some children keep their rooms in an extremely untidy and even unclean condition. When parents demand that they clean it up, some of these children respond, "But it's *my* room." In a way, these children have a point, unless, however, they have peanut butter and jelly sandwiches growing mold under their beds. Sometimes I think it would be helpful if the Board of Health were to establish some minimum standard of neatness and cleanliness for children's rooms. Unfortunately, however, there is no law that will help parents at present.

The state of children's rooms is an age-old, probably unresolvable conflict between parents and children. The best approach in this no-win situation is to use ingenuity to avoid confrontations where either or both of you can lose face.

Teenagers, whose rooms can sometimes resemble disaster areas, may be simply asserting themselves and rebelling against your insistence that they clean up. I think it's important to avoid a screaming fight, since that will only strengthen the youngster's resolve to be messy and further frustrate you. If your child steadfastly refuses to tidy up, I think it's best to work out a solution when all seems well and communication is at its best. Don't hesitate to express your frustration about the problem. Ask your teenager for help in finding a solution. You can say, "I love you and I think you're a wonderful person—I only wish you could help me work out a way to solve this problem, which is interfering with our relationship." By appealing in this way, you are taking constructive steps toward solving the difficulty and also helping your child understand that human beings can get frustrated—and that even parents sometimes need the help of their children in resolving problems.

Perhaps it will help parents keep a realistic perspective on this sort of situation if they know that there are some people who are *too* neat. People who are obsessive-compulsive require everything to be neat and clean, symmetrical, and not moved from the assigned place. Probably everyone knows someone like this—someone who has covers on the furniture and covers on the covers, who must keep all the window shades perfectly even. Such people are generally "uptight" in other ways as well. They make wonderful housekeepers but find it difficult to tolerate children. That's why I frequently point out to parents that they can hire someone to care for the children, and/or someone to care for the house, but rarely one person to do both. The qualities that make someone work hard to keep a house extremely neat and clean and orderly are usually the qualities that make someone restrict children so much that they cannot exercise their natural ability to explore, play, or be creative.

MODEL CHILD
(SEE ALSO *Discipline and Punishment, Obedience*)

When parents are too demanding with children and set severe limits on their freedom, children can become extremely submissive. Overly constricting limits can stifle a child's curiosity, and he may soon find learning an unpleasant process. While most parents want their children to be obedient, the *totally* obedient child may have given up on his curiosity. He frequently shows little interest in expressing himself and is often hesitant to carry out any task unless it is clearly requested and outlined by others. Such children often grow up to be passive individuals lacking in drive, imagination, and initiative; they seem satisfied to follow through on the wishes of others. Sometimes the model child reaches a point where he is unable to suppress his own ideas and feelings any longer, and may abruptly shift from being a model child to being the neighborhood terror.

Parents and teachers often like model children because they make no demands and they are easy to handle. However, when they hold such children up as examples by saying, "Jennifer does everything *she's* told," or "Watch Michael and see how you *should* behave," model children become the target of their siblings' or peers' anger about such comparisons. Model children are often teased by other children, or even rejected. Such a youngster can have an unhappy childhood. Under the heading DISCIPLINE AND PUNISHMENT I suggest more appropriate ways to establish and ensure that, while they may be generally obedient, children should also be allowed to express their own feelings, to act on their own initiative, and to grow emotionally.

MOOD
(SEE ALSO *Adolescence*)

Everyone has good and bad moods. It's important for parents to recognize this and to communicate to their children when they're feeling irritable or tired that "right now I'm just in a bad mood." This can help a child understand that she herself did not provoke this negative behavior on your part. It can help a child understand that after a hard day at the office, or some other difficulty, you are not as receptive to her as you would otherwise be. Usually, saying "I'm in a good mood," or "I'm in a bad mood" doesn't require any further explanation.

Some people do indeed have mood swings that are extreme, which are technically called manic-depressive. When these mood swings have a pattern and are profound, frequently they are related to biochemical factors in the body. Hormonal changes account for mood swings, as many women know. Premenstrual tension is a recognized concept that has even been given legal recognition in accounting for mood changes. Some time ago in Britain, premenstrual stress was accepted as a mitigating circumstance in the sentencing of two women accused of violent crimes. Another example is the emotional and behavioral changes that we see in an emerging adolescent as hormones begin to flow through the body, causing emotional and physical changes. Consequently we see more mood swings and erratic feelings in teenagers. Some people being treated with hormones for certain illnesses also experience mood changes. Among diabetics, a change in blood sugar level during various times of the day can account for irritability, sleepiness, or anger. Frequently, people who seem to have an addiction to sweets show marked mood changes when their blood sugar level drops, and seem to need something with sugar in it almost as a "fix" to get them back to a level of amiability. If this occurs in your child, it is wise to consult a pediatrician to see if the child has a problem with blood sugar or diabetes, or a hormonal problem.

MOTHER

(SEE ALSO *Babysitter, Day Care, Family, Father, Oedipus Complex*)

Biological factors make the mother-child relationship unique. Only the female can nurture new life within her body, feel new life moving and kicking inside her own body, feed her baby with milk from her own body. As countless works of art through the ages have illustrated, the loving expression of a mother when she holds her newborn child is a beautiful sight. For many women, even for many little girls, one of the greatest desires in life is to become a mother.

Are pregnancy, childbirth, and breastfeeding then the essence of motherhood? Far from it. Many mothers do not have all these experiences: many women become mothers through adoption, many feed their babies with bottles. In terms of time, the processes of pregnancy, childbirth, and breastfeeding are a relatively small part of motherhood. And many women, to whatever degree they enjoy these processes, derive their greatest satisfaction from other aspects of motherhood—from childrearing rather than childbearing and nursing.

Today, most mothers work outside the home as well as in it. It can be extremely gratifying to combine childrearing with another career, and it can be extremely difficult. The situation can be enormously facilitated when fathers share in the traditionally female activities of childcare and housekeeping, and when employers provide some flexibility.

I believe that fathers and mothers should share all responsibilities for the care and raising of children. In fact, I see nothing wrong with fathers staying at home, taking primary responsibility for the care of children, while mothers go off to work. I have encountered more and more arrangements like this in recent years, since the number of women in the work force has increased.

I must say that when both parents of *small* children work full-time outside the home, this causes me deep concern. Children under the age of three need a great deal of parental time and attention. I have seen many adult patients with substantial emotional problems who have never gotten over the lack of self-importance that came from having been raised by a succession of caretakers.

I fervently advocate that business and government organizations accommodate themselves to mothers who work. I see no reason why they cannot offer flexible working hours, split jobs, or time during the middle of the day to help mothers assume their family responsibilities. Ideally, such an arrangement should be available to fathers as well, so that either parent—or both—could spend a few hours in the middle of the day with their baby or young child.

With older children, it would be helpful to have one parent at home when the children arrive after school. If this is not possible, the parents should attempt to arrange some afterschool activities for their children. At the very least, parents should telephone the children to ask how things went during the day.

If a mother is returning to work after her children are older— perhaps in their pre-teen years—their reaction to this situation will depend greatly on the kind of emotional investment that has been made in them in the previous years. Children who accept such changes with little difficulty are those whose parents respected them as individuals and who assisted them in developing their own resources for coping with life's problems at each stage of their development.

Whatever the amount of time spent with children, if they feel that they are truly loved by and important to their parents, mothers and fathers will have accomplished the most important things they can do.

MOVING
(SEE ALSO *Regression*)

Moving, even if it's just a few miles away, can be difficult for a child. After all, a child's world is small. If she's very young, just moving from one block to another may mean she no longer sees her best chum, the one who was so good at making mudpies; maybe now there's a big dog with a big bark next door; certainly her new room has new shadows at night. I remember one three-year-old who, when approached in her new home by a would-be playmate, repeatedly reacted by putting her head down and plaintively saying, "Go away." By the fascinating process of a three-year-old mind, she was trying to re-establish her old home and her old relationships. By telling people to go away, she was reacting as if the move had not taken place.

With an older child, there are even more adjustments. In addition to a new home, new neighborhood and new friends, there is a new school. Many books for children begin with a family's moving from one place to another; in most of these books, as in life, however adventurous a child, she feels some sense of loss and some trepidation about the new and unknown.

Parents can do a lot to help children deal with these feelings. If you yourself are apprehensive or upset about the move, it's best to say it outright. Your children will certainly sense it. You can then concentrate on making the best of an imperfect situation. Let your children know that you understand that things will be somewhat different, that it will be sort of sad to move away from the surroundings with which the family is familiar, that it will take a while to get used to all the new things and new people. But you can also tell your children that they can write letters to their old friends. Perhaps —depending on how far the move is—your children can plan to call their old friends on the phone or even exchange visits with them now and then. You can help your children realize that no move has to be a complete rupture with the past.

You can also stress the adventurous aspects of the move. After all, this is an exciting opportunity for the whole family to broaden their horizons, meet new people, and do new things. Emphasize your confidence that your family will become as much a part of the new neighborhood as you were of the old. Sometimes children become more excited and positive about a move if they visit the new community beforehand, just to get an impression of where they're going.

Once you move, it can be very helpful if you yourself make an effort to become active in the new community, particularly if you make friendly overtures toward people whose children are the same age as yours. By seeing you interact with these new people, your children will feel safer in reaching out to establish new friendships.

N

NAPS
(SEE ALSO *Sleep*)

Most babies and young children need to have daytime naps. Parents sometimes try to have a child skip a nap to encourage an earlier bedtime. This rarely works. More often than not, the child who misses a nap becomes irritable and doesn't necessarily go to bed earlier.

When a child is close to three years of age, he may no longer need a nap, but during the transitional period between needing and not needing a nap, a parent goes through some anguish because of the child's passing irritability. Once the child is solidly past his need for a nap, life becomes easier for everyone.

NEUROLOGICAL DISTURBANCES
(SEE ALSO *Accident Prone, Hyperactivity, Language Development Problems, Retardation, Stuttering*)

Behavioral disturbances frequently are caused by a dysfunction of the nervous system—the brain and all the connecting nerves. This physiological problem is sometimes so subtle that doctors do not observe it during a routine physical examination. Dysfunction of the nervous system can be caused by brain or spinal injuries, by viruses that inflame various parts of the brain; by certain chemical imbalances, including lead poisoning and malnutrition; or by a number of complications, including lack of oxygen, that can occur during childbirth.

If a child exhibits behavioral problems such as severe temper tantrums, learning difficulties, or hyperactivity, it is vitally important to diagnose the cause. Are the problems primarily the result of environmental factors—that is, circumstances in his life at present or in his early upbringing? Or are they the result of physiological factors—such as a neurological disorder?

The reason it is so important to determine the root of the problem is that the treatment required for environmental factors is different from the treatment for physiological factors. A child whose disturbed behavior is due to some central nervous system dysfunction often develops an emotional problem in addition to his physiological problem. For example, his slow learning causes classmates to ridicule or reject him, which contributes to his failing in school, and he subsequently feels inadequate or insecure. A psychologist can treat the "superimposed" emotional problem without ever alleviating the underlying physiological cause. In my opinion this is too often the case. The majority of children with central nervous system dysfunction who suffer from poor concentration and hyperactivity frequently can be treated with medication, and sometimes additionally with psychotherapy and dietary changes.

I want to point out one very important thing: a child with some dysfunction of the nervous system or even one with brain damage is *not* necessarily emotionally disturbed or intellectually limited. In fact, I have diagnosed many of these children and have found many to be intellectually gifted. Further, many such children are happy and well-adjusted. They have learned to cope with their physiological problem in much the same way a person with a deformity learns to compensate for his defect. Of course, how much a child can adapt depends to some extent on the degree of nervous system dysfunction.

How do you know whether your child has such a physiological problem? Signs sometimes appear subtly between four and six months of age. Babies who have a strange cry, show little or no eye contact, or have poor muscle tone (sometimes called "floppy baby") may be suffering from a physically-based behavioral problem.

Parents often ask me whether a child who is slow in developing has some sort of learning problem. I usually tell mothers and fathers not to compare their children with other children in regard to "milestones in development," since all children are different and are on different timetables. Unquestionably, consult your pediatrician to determine if your child's development is abnormal, but keep in mind that minor lags in development may simply be due to individual differences.

The major behavioral disturbances of many children who find themselves in trouble in school center on learning problems. A child may have a short attention span, difficulty concentrating, or difficulty reading or writing. Some children are defiant, rebellious, or unwilling to do what the teacher says. Frequently, a child's disturbed behavior is evidence of some minor brain damage. Unrecognized and untreated, the damage may lead to secondary or superimposed emotional difficulties.

Sometimes a child's disturbed behavior can be a sign of a brain tumor. Severe headaches, dizziness, staggering, together with vomiting and lack of muscle control or the inability to use muscles, sometimes signal the possibility of a brain tumor. Be wary of psychological explanations of the symptoms until an experienced neurologist checks them out. Other signs of neurological disturbances are convulsions and loss of consciousness. Consult a neurologist about these symptoms as well.

I would urge parents to seek professional help if they suspect that their child's difficulties fit into any of these patterns. Too many parents try to go it alone, or worse yet, to deny that a problem exists. While I think it is important for you to try to deal with your child's difficulty, it is better to have professional help to solve the problem.

NEUROSIS
(SEE ALSO *Accident Prone, Aggression, Anorexia Nervosa, Bedwetting, Cheating, Daydreaming, Depression, Fears, Guilt, Juvenile Delinquency, Neurological Disturbances, Obesity, Separation Anxiety, Sleep, Soiling, Stealing, Toilet Training*)

Neuroses, sometimes called psychoneuroses, are the result of internalized conflicts which are entirely or partly outside a person's conscious awareness. The primary means of keeping these conflicts out of awareness is by repressing unacceptable thoughts and ideas. By making the thoughts unconscious, a person avoids unpleasant feelings and tensions. In a neurosis, the attempt to repress the idea fails, and symptoms and problems in adjustment occur.

Rarely do we see a neurotic disorder in children under the age of four or five, because the mental structure is not sufficiently developed to allow internal conflict of any significance to develop. Neurotic conflicts can occur at different levels in the form of conscious worries; feelings of guilt; irrational fears; and disturbing thoughts, fantasies, and wishes. We sometimes see an exaggeration of certain sensory or motor functions, such as a loss of speech, blindness, or bedwetting (beyond a certain age). We sometimes see ulcers in children as a sign of neurosis.

Some forms of neurosis are characterized by intense anxiety, which can cause overeating, sleep disturbances, and such habits as severe nail biting. Sometimes the anxiety is very specific, and the child develops a fear of something special, or of a certain situation. This fear is called a phobia. Phobias occur normally at certain times in development. A phobia, in a sense, is an irrational fear of great intensity, such as a fear of going to school. While the child may claim that he's afraid of other children or of the teacher, the underlying cause may be fear of leaving his home. Some children are fearful that something serious might happen when they are away from home.

Another category of neurosis is what is called an obsessive-compulsive problem. This is basically a persistent and repetitious thought, generally recognized by the child as being beyond his control. For example, the child may fear that the parent is going to die. This fear can be complicated by certain rituals the child feels he must perform to avoid the death of his parent. It's not unlike the children's game and chant, "Step on a crack and you break your mother's back." Basically, the obsessive-compulsive ritual serves to keep the unpleasant thoughts and feelings from coming into consciousness.

Depression can be another manifestation of neurosis.

Still other neurotic manifestations are called "acting out" disorders. Here a child gives vent to impulses without any awareness of what his behavior means to others. These behaviors may be, for example, unprovoked aggression, stealing, or sexual impulses expressed destructively. This kind of anti-social behavior is frequently referred to as "delinquency."

Some children who are *constantly* having accidents, falling down, or hurting themselves are considered "accident prone," and this can be a neurotic manifestation if neurological dysfunction is ruled out as a cause.

Some neurotic conflicts manifest themselves in learning problems, which are caused by a preoccupation with certain ideas, due to repressed anger and aggression. Learning problems are sometimes due to the distraction of daydreams that interfere with the ability to concentrate.

Enuresis (bedwetting) is an involuntary discharge of urine that occurs well beyond the age when bladder control should have been developed (this control is generally not established until a child is between two and three, and in some instances between five and six years of age). Soiling (encopresis) beyond the age of four or five years may represent a neurotic disorder. This behavior generally reflects a more serious kind of disturbance in the parent/child relationship. It's generally related to problems during bowel training.

NUDITY
(SEE ALSO *Pornography*)

I have always believed that parents should be casual with their children about nudity. However, this does not mean I recommend that parents be exhibitionists and walk about in a provocative manner. Children in the course of their own growth will develop feelings of modesty about themselves and also about their parents. This will probably mean that even though you may have started out being casual with toddlers and preschoolers, you may eventually discover that your children prefer to leave the room when you're nude, and that they close the door when they're bathing or undressing.

O

OBESITY
(SEE ALSO *Appetite, Food*)

Some children are overweight because of a medical problem such as a metabolic disorder. You should consult your pediatrician to find any possible physical cause for your child's obesity. If, however, a child has an inordinate appetite, and seemingly no physical problem, then you might consider a psychological evaluation to see if her overeating is due to an emotional problem. Many people who eat insatiably feel unloved, and their overeating is an attempt to gain love. There is an unconscious association between the intake of food and the feeling of being loved, since in early infancy love and attention were part of the feeding process.

You should offer your child help and support in losing weight. Some parents think that teasing obese children will get them to take off pounds, but nagging and ridicule serve no good purpose whatsoever and can lead to feelings of rejection, compounding the problem. Children who are teased often feel inadequate, which causes them to eat more in defiance of their parents or as a means of gaining emotional satisfaction.

Of course, it would seem unfair to deprive one child of cakes and ice cream while her siblings are allowed to eat to their hearts' content. Ideally, you should try to keep tempting food out of her sight. This can best be done by changing the entire family's diet. It is possible to plan meals for your whole family that will be tasty yet low in calories. Children who enjoy sweets can learn to be satisfied with fruit, especially if you keep a supply of it—rather than cookies and high-calorie snacks—in the house. It is important, however, to make it clear that you are modifying these eating habits for the entire family's benefit, as a means of preventing health problems for everyone in the future. This will protect your overweight child from the rejection of her brothers and sisters, who may blame her for these changes.

One twelve-year-old girl I know joined Weight Watchers on her own. She said two things helped her make that decision: "First of all, my mother took me to a doctor and he told me that I weighed too much and he explained that it wasn't healthy. But I guess I really wanted to lose weight because I couldn't fit into a lot of clothes that I wanted to wear, pants and stuff." This young woman reinforced the idea that the decision to diet must be a personal one: "Parents who support their kid's desire to lose weight are great, but they have to realize that it's something you have to do for yourself, not for anyone else."

OBSCENITY

There is no way you can control the language your child uses in all situations. Parents can certainly set an example for children by refraining from cursing in their presence. But children may pick up vulgar language from TV or movies, or from playmates or peers, or from other adults. We can't always assume that children understand the words they're using. However, children often will repeat these obscenities in front of adults in order to shock them or to get attention. I think that if you are very harsh or punitive on this issue, you may intensify your child's use of the words and make them more important than they are.

Probably the best way to handle it is to point out matter-of-factly that you do not carry on conversations when those words are used and you know that people you respect behave in the same way. If, however, you *do* use profanity in your speech, you can say that you do not think it is appropriate for children to use such langauge. You also might consider allowing your children to curse at home, but not elsewhere. Many parents react to cursing by announcing, "I never want to hear you use that kind of language at home!" Well, if you can't feel comfortable in your own home, where can you feel comfortable? It may make more sense to tell your children to use that sort of language in the privacy of home, but not anyplace else! It all depends on how you feel about vulgar language, whether you use it yourself, and how strongly you feel about your children's using it.

OEDIPUS COMPLEX
(SEE ALSO *Incest, Jealousy*)

The Oedipus complex is the term developed by Freud to refer to the attachment between a mother and son. It has its origin in the Greek myth in which the King of Thebes left his son Oedipus to die when it was predicted that the child would grow up to kill him. Oedipus was saved, and when he met his father—without knowing his identity—he killed him in an argument. Afterward, Oedipus married his widowed mother without knowing that she was his mother. The term Electra complex is sometimes used to refer to a similar attachment between father and daughter. Basically, the psychodynamics are the same as in the mother-son relationship. Electra was the daughter of King Agamemnon. She and her brother Orestes killed their mother Clytemnestra after Clytemnestra and her lover killed the king.

The so-called Oedipus complex reflects the stage of development that manifests itself in a boy's strong positive feelings for his mother, and consequent anger and resentment toward his father. When a three- to five-year-old boy tells his mother, "Mommy, I'm going to marry you when I grow up," this is a natural reflection of the boy's going through this developmental stage.

However, sometimes a boy's strong feelings persist beyond the normal time for this developmental stage. Sometimes a mother encourages this strong tie, because of an unsatisfactory marital situation, perhaps a divorce, or perhaps because the mother enjoys the kind of role this involves. Sometimes a mother allows her son to become a wedge between mother and father. If a boy's attachment to his mother is extremely strong, and if it continues, this can create major problems. Later on, the growing child may be unable to make attachments to other people, to establish a clear gender identification, or to avoid sexual confusion and guilt. It is best if parents are affectionate with and close to one another throughout their child's development. It is best if parents do not allow a child to come between them—even though they are devoted to the child's physical and emotional welfare. In this way, the child will feel secure in the love of both mother and father. It will also serve as a model of adult behavior that will motivate him to seek a satisfying sexual and emotional relationship with a person in the image of his father's choice—that is, a loving person like his mother.

ONLY CHILD
(SEE ALSO *Sibling*)

There is no reason at all why you can't bring up an only child to be well adjusted, well liked, and respectful of other people's feelings. In fact, an only child is likely to get a good deal of individual time and attention, which is so essential to the emotional health of children during their early years. If anyone tells you that you should give your child a sibling as a companion or a friend, you can point out that not only is that insufficient reason for having a second child, but for every only child who wished for a brother or sister there are probably at least a dozen children with siblings who wished they were only children.

If you are concerned that your child learn how to share, the experience of nursery school should provide plenty of opportunities for this. When children interact with one another, they develop internal controls and a tolerance for frustration that helps them become better socialized and capable of dealing with freedom; but such learning experiences are not limited to families with brothers and sisters.

There have certainly been only children who have been spoiled, indulged, and catered to. But this can happen to any child, regardless of whether he has siblings or not.

OVERPROTECTIVENESS
(SEE ALSO *Adolescence, Fears, Independence, Individuality, Smothering Parent*)

When parents repeatedly warn children of hazards that may occur, children will feel uncomfortable away from the parents. Such parents can inhibit children's curiosity about the way the world works and make them overly dependent—or defiant and rebellious. Children should be taught mastery of their environment, not fear of it. Otherwise they will never feel competent or confident, and they will never really mature.

I find that it is generally parents who are fearful themselves who tend to pass on their anxieties to their children. Sometimes such parents unconsciously need to keep their children close to them and dependent on them. I recall one mother of a four-year-old boy who requested an emergency appointment with me because of her son's fearfulness and dependency. When I walked into the waiting room I found the little boy playing quite contentedly on the floor with some toys. I said, "Richard, do you mind if I talk with your mother?" He looked up, smiled, and shook his head. Richard's mother then rose. "Richard," she said, "Everything will be all right." Richard continued to play. "There's nothing to worry about," the mother said. Richard kept on playing. "Richard, do you hear me?" his mother said. In an urgent voice she repeated, "Everything will be all right!" With this, Richard grabbed his mother's ankle and began to scream. The mother looked at me and said, with a smile, "See? That's my problem!" She was correct. It was *her* problem. She needed to maintain control of her child. She feared his becoming independent of her, and so encouraged his dependence on her.

It is important for parents to prepare their children to meet the world as it is, and to be able to deal with it. Parents who overprotect their children handicap them, in a sense, by limiting their opportunities to explore, and thus to learn about the world and about their own place in it. Often, overprotected children become shy, passive, and withdrawn, afraid to become involved, afraid to take risks, afraid of anything new. Or conversely, they may become defiant or rebellious. If parents avoid either overprotecting their children or pushing them into experiences for which the children do not feel ready, the children will be able to learn for themselves about the world, and about their own capabilities.

If parents are truthful with their children, the children will trust them. But if parents tell their children, "Masturbation will make you crazy," or "All people who aren't just like us are dangerous," or otherwise lie or grossly exaggerate the dangers of the world when their children are young, they should not expect their children to believe them when they are adolescents.

It is particularly important for parents to avoid overprotecting their adolescents. It is some parents' inability to see their children grow up and become independent of them that leads many teenagers to react by becoming defiant and rebellious. Parents who allow their adolescents the flexibility and freedom to grow and to learn are helping their children to become adults.

P

PACIFIER
(SEE ALSO *Breastfeeding, Instincts, Sucking, Weaning*)

A pacifier is a device like a nipple that is placed in a baby's mouth and which frequently quiets her by providing an object for her to suck on.

While I am inclined to advise against using a pacifier, I am not absolutely opposed to them. If a child is in the hospital or ill or suffering in some way, a pacifier can be very reassuring. But I am opposed to putting a pacifier into a child's mouth the instant she cries. Often babies cry because they need cuddling and play, and using a pacifier means the baby is "plugged up" and not picked up. If this happens, an infant may be getting less of the cuddling and sensory stimulation that is so important for healthy emotional development.

Giving an infant a pacifier every time she cries is not unlike giving an adult a tranquilizer every time he feels unhappy. It is far better to help your infant by finding out what is causing her to cry than to increase the use of the sucking response as the means for reducing anxiety. I do feel that sucking should be gratified—but in a functional way, with the intake of food. Instead of giving your child a pacifier, perhaps you should give her a bottle with water or fruit juice.

Another reason for avoiding the pacifier is this: research has revealed that babies show less exploratory visual behavior while sucking on a pacifier than they would if a pacifier were not available. Since an infant learns a great deal about her environment by visual exploration, the pacifier may cut down the external information your baby receives. Because your child has a need to be picked up and to move around, giving her a pacifier every time she is uncomfortable tends to reinforce the use of some kind of oral stimulation in place of the other kinds of stimulation your infant needs.

If your child is dependent on the pacifier it will be somewhat of a disappointment to her to have to give it up. If she still takes the bottle, you might simply take the pacifier away and let her have the bottle at the times when she wants the pacifier. On the other hand, if your child is older, verbal, and no longer on the breast or bottle, when you want to "wean" her from the pacifier I suggest you tell her that she can "have it today and tomorrow and the next day— and then no more." Each succeeding day remind her that in a short time she will no longer be having it. This preparation doesn't mean that she will willingly give up the pacifier when the times comes. You can be almost certain that she will be somewhat upset and angry when she finally learns that what you have told her is true. (Be sure you stick to your word!) At that time it is important not to return the pacifier but to offer her additional cuddling and comforting.

PERMISSIVENESS
(SEE ALSO *Discipline and Punishment*)

Unfortunately, some people believe that the absence of rules and regulations for their children facilitates a sense of freedom. This is not true. Children need rules and regulations to guide their behavior as long as these rules do not restrict them from being able to express themselves or have choices. Without some guidance of this kind, children frequently feel that parents do not care.

Everyone needs to learn to channel his feelings and actions in a socially acceptable way. By not setting limits, you not only create anxiety and encourage destructiveness, you can lead your child to feel that you don't care at *all* what he does. This not only makes him feel unimportant but also can lead him to do things that are socially unacceptable while wishing someone who loves him would care enough to stop him. No one wants to be in the company of a destructive child. By allowing a child to be destructive and function without limits you are, in effect, curtailing his freedom.

On the other hand, some children reared in an atmosphere of permissiveness become terribly inhibited. It's important to remember that there is no such thing as "freedom" unless there are limits. Freedom requires boundaries or else it becomes "not caring." In the same way that the word "yes" would have no meaning in a language that lacks the word "no," so does freedom have no meaning unless there are limits concerning what is acceptable behavior.

PETS
(SEE ALSO *Death*)

Caring for a pet can be a very positive emotional experience for a child. Having responsibility for a pet not only provides children with the opportunity for taking on a role that prepares them for life's responsibilities, pleasures, and commitments, but it also teaches them sensitivity and helps them try out some of the important experiences that will ultimately be beneficial for their adult human interactions.

Sometimes children who have pent-up anger direct it at pets and they can be rather cruel. If this occurs, it should be a message to you that your child has emotions that need release. You should find out whether it is anger or frustration he is venting, or merely roughhouse playing. In either case, you should intervene on behalf of the animal, making it clear to your child that animals have feelings too.

The death of a pet offers a natural opportunity for teaching a child about death and how to cope with such a loss. With all good intentions many parents want to protect their children from the reality of death, but this is something that will have to be faced sooner or later. I know it is difficult to explain an abstract concept like death in concrete terms to a young child. But she will probably want to know specific things such as why a person or pet can no longer do the things he used to do and why parents and doctors can't do anything about it. The death of your pet should be explained as "like being broken and no one can fix things again—not even the doctor." You can add, "this can happen because of a serious accident or sickness—or when you are very, very old." This will be more comprehensible to a child than if she were told, "God took your dog away and he is in heaven." Then you are sure to be faced with such questions as "Why did God take him away and will God give my dog back?" It is not right to tell your child that death is like being asleep for a long, long time. This explanation may easily result in a fear of going to sleep.

After explaining the death of a pet you might suggest getting another family animal, even though no dog (cat, lizard, turtle, fish) can ever really replace Fido. Ask your child to take part in choosing a new pet.

Often children beg for an animal, promise to care for it, and then forget about their responsibility. You should not allow this to happen. If your child agrees to feed, walk, and clean up after his pet, make certain that he lives up to his agreement. If he does not, you should sit down with him and in a calm, businesslike manner tell him that you have decided to give up the pet for adoption. Explain that you have reached this decision after careful evaluation of the situation and want to place the matter before him to see if he has any other suggestions that will be acceptable to you. Have ready in the back of your mind a suggestion that is acceptable—one that gives back to the child the primary responsibility for caring for his pet—and be prepared to play your part in firmly enforcing this policy.

PLAY
(SEE ALSO *Curiosity, Dropping Things, Friends, Learning*)

Play serves an extremely important function in a child's learning about the world. As a child begins to move around and develop motor coordination, his play—which is really his work throughout his childhood—enables him to exercise his muscles as well as his imagination. From the very beginning various objects in his environment, as well as toys, provide the stimulation needed to do this—mobiles to look at, music boxes to listen to, stuffed toys to touch and feel, rubber rings to gum, chew, taste, and smell. In a stimulus-rich environment a baby can perceive and respond, and will generally crave more stimulation to find out how things work and what impact his behavior has. He does this by pushing and pulling, opening and shutting, taking out and putting in, building up and knocking down.

In the beginning of this phase the child enjoys these play activities purely for their own sake. Later, play becomes more purposeful. The child looks for cause and effect; that is, he tries to discover what makes things happen and whether these things happen all the time. He does something for the sake of an end result. He is learning and enjoying the challenges which help him complete a task and enjoy solving problems, and which will later on help him develop positive work habits. This, together with enjoying the reactions of adults from whom he learns—first his parents and later his teachers—is the basis for increased motivation for learning and can set the stage for doing well in school.

I should note that while young children have a real need for play materials they can manipulate and handle, such objects needn't be expensive commercial toys; household implements will do. Babies and young children love to play with "real" things—bunches of keys, flashlights, pots and pans, egg beaters and wooden cooking spoons from the kitchen, handbags and hats from the closet. These things have the added attraction of belonging to Mommy and Daddy —or being just like the ones that do—and they make it easier for the child's imagination to bridge the gap between the reality of his being small and the pretense of being big that is such an important part of learning what it's really like to be big.

Because play is so important to a child's development, I believe toys and play materials should be considered almost as necessary as food and clothing. Therefore, they shouldn't be used for disciplinary purposes, or as a reward. Children get bored without objects to play with; this can hamper the learning process.

Aside from alleviating boredom and expanding knowledge about how things work in the world, play allows children to attain a certain awareness of how their actions affect other people and why they must show some degree of restraint. For instance, very young children don't realize at first that other children are creatures like themselves. They seem to think of them as things—objects that are sometimes convenient, and sometimes a nuisance. Repeated exposure to these other children soon reveals that they are creatures who also hurt when they are hit (they cry) and even hit back (so perhaps one shouldn't provoke them?).

PORNOGRAPHY
(SEE ALSO *Adolescence, Nudity, Sex Education, Sexual Experiences*)

As strong sexual feelings emerge during adolescence, many young people display an interest in sexually explicit books, magazines, and movies. If you have always had a frank, open, and trusting relationship with your youngster, there is no reason for it to end now. You should express your feelings about this subject. First, however, do let your youngster know that it is perfectly normal for boys and girls alike to be strongly interested in sex, particularly when they are in the process of becoming men and women, and sexual activity is new to them. You can let them know that later they may be more inclined to view sex within the context of a rich and complex relationship between two people, while still seeing it as a uniquely pleasurable experience.

If you disapprove of sexually explicit material, it would be helpful to your children if you told them the reason for your disapproval. For example, if you believe that sexually explicit magazines treat people as sex objects rather than human beings, point this out. If you believe that it distorts human experience and human nature to isolate this one aspect of life, say so.

PRAISE
(SEE ALSO *Acceptance, Approval, Criticism, Discipline and Punishment, Rewards*)

Giving a child praise can go a long way toward increasing his sense of self-esteem and responsibility. Children need to be rewarded by parental approval and recognition; they need to feel—as we all do—that their behavior and reactions are meaningful to people, particularly those who love them and set limits on their behavior in the form of disciplining them. Without such rewards, a child can lose his motivation to please others and may begin to fail at school. His attitude may be one of "I couldn't care less what things mean to other people." By giving praise to a child for a job well done, you will encourage him to further his endeavors. On the other hand, if you discourage him, ignore him, or are constantly critical of his abilities, you may be denying him the opportunity to make his mark on the world.

It's important to remember that praise must be given honestly, and be justified. Simply praising a child to make him feel better without his having warranted the praise is neither honest nor sincere and can weaken the meaning of justifiable praise.

PREMATURITY, DEALING WITH
(SEE ALSO *Childbirth, Infancy*)

Since most expectant parents anticipate having a full-term baby, having a premature baby can come as a shock that can cause feelings of guilt. These guilty feelings can lead to a great deal of self-examination: "What did I do that was wrong?" "What did I eat?" "What did I drink?" These questions are common, and perfectly understandable. Although it is not completely clear as to why babies are premature, some of the causes are known. Drugs, cigarettes, and alcohol are all detrimental to an unborn baby. Diabetes is also connected to premature births. Sometimes there are anatomical problems, such as a low-lying placenta that blocks the opening of the uterus and prevents a normal birth. Expectant mothers can avoid potential problems by eliminating drugs, cigarettes, and alcohol as well as by maintaining proper nutrition.

The important thing to remember after a baby's premature birth is that premature babies need as much cuddling, love, and stimulation as full-term babies—and perhaps a little bit more to compensate for the forced separation during the time the tiny infant is kept in an incubator. While the incubator is necessary for the baby's physical health, it can be mentally stressful for a premature infant. Researchers are discovering that the harsh glare of fluorescent lights and the constant din of machinery in a premature nursery can be hard on a child. That, combined with the relative lack of human contact, causes parents to worry, and rightfully so, I think. Some hospitals are making an effort to ease this situation—turning down the lights at night, redesigning incubators to make them quieter, and allowing parents to reach in and touch their babies, perhaps even take them out for short periods of time for feeding when the baby is physically able to handle it. One approach to perinatal care involves bringing premature infants together as often as possible not only with their mothers, but with the rest of the family—fathers, siblings, and grandparents. After the mother goes home, but the baby is still not ready to leave the hospital, this new approach encourages family members to come back to the hospital and spend as much time as possible with the baby. This approach is not only helpful to the babies, it is also helpful in alleviating the anxieties of mothers and other family members.

While there is no reason to think that premature babies will have any particular emotional problems later in childhood, they may have some difficulties. In some cases, premature babies are more sensitive to light and sound and tend to become irritated more easily. However, we do know that babies who get a lot of cuddling seem to be more outgoing, independent, and friendly later in life. Like full-term babies, "preemies" can flourish emotionally if their parents cultivate a trusting, loving relationship with them early in life.

PRIVACY

As a rule, children learn to respect the privacy of others, including their parents, when parents themselves respect others' privacy, including their children's. For example, it is important for parents to knock on their children's bedroom doors before entering, and to refrain from opening their children's mail. When parents tell their children, "I don't want to interrupt you if you're in the middle of something," they offer an excellent example of respecting the privacy of others.

If children have difficulty respecting their parents' privacy—if, for example, they repeatedly interrupt their parents' conversations, or expect that their parents drop whatever they're doing and help with homework, parents and children can discuss this issue together. As always, it's best to do so when all is well and communication is at its height, which is of course rarely the case at the moment of crisis.

However, parents should keep in mind that their lives will never be as private as the lives of non-parents. The commitment to parenthood means living with the reality of children's behavior. This includes periods of impulsivity and impatience, and issues of great urgency—such as the need to rush an ailing gerbil to the vet, zoom to the hobby shop for a particular kind of World War I biplane, or offer consolation on the tearful announcement, "My best friend hates my guts!"

The only way a parent will get "tea for two" is if she is trying to read *War and Peace* or trying to write her department's five-year plan, and a four-year-old in pigtails comes in and pours what is actually apple juice into tiny plastic cups that are not even close to clean. Then the parent must stop what she is doing, take a sip, and say, "Mmmm. This tastes delicious. It's just what I needed." And strangly enough, sometimes it is just what the parent needed. Sometimes when parents' solemn adult activities are interrupted by children who offer a cup of tea, that innocent and beautiful moment reminds them of why they chose to have children instead of complete privacy.

157

R

REASONING
(SEE ALSO *Discipline and Punishment*)

Parents who reason with their children demonstrate a respect for that child as a person.

On the other hand, reasoning with a very young child—a two-year-old, for instance—can be ineffective. It is better for parents to demonstrate their feelings to a toddler rather than to recount the reasons why they are displeased with his behavior. It is fairly meaningless to a two-year-old child to hear his parents say calmly and dispassionately, "We are very angry and upset with you because you have thrown your cup of milk on the floor several times today. Yes, it's true. We are very angry indeed." If parents clearly show their annoyance with their facial expression and tone of voice, it would be far more effective. It is only when a child is a little older that the expression of your feelings, accompanied by a literal explanation, will help the child feel, as well as intellectually understand, the consequences of his actions.

REASSURANCE

(SEE ALSO *Death, Divorce, Hospitalization, Illness, Moving, Regression, Sibling, Teething*)

There are many times in a child's life when unpredictable events such as illness, separation, death, divorce, injury, and accidents occur. Generally speaking, children feel comfortable when "all is well" and nothing out of the ordinary takes place. If something unexpectedly unpleasant occurs the child feels anxious and vulnerable. He may feel a sense of betrayal since his "all powerful" parents were unable to protect him. This leads him to anticipate more unpredictable or stressful events. Assurance and reassurance that he will be helped is necessary to allay his fears of more impending trouble. Without reassurance, a child can hardly mobilize his resources to cope with unpleasantness in a manner that enables him to feel he has mastered the problem and now has the skill to cope better when another problem arises.

REBELLION

(SEE ALSO *Adolescence, Alcohol and Drug Abuse Among Teenagers, Defiance, Discipline and Punishment, Independence, Individuality*)

In our culture it is very difficult for some teenagers to achieve independence without rebelling against the people on whom they have been dependent—their parents. The anthropologist Margaret Mead found that adolescent rebellion does not exist in all societies; in cultures where teenagers could make the transition from childhood to adulthood easily and quickly, with acceptance and support from the adult members of that community, rebelliousness either did not occur or was minimal. The "rites of passage" or other rituals that young people go through in some primitive societies help them make that transition cleanly and quickly, thus avoiding the long period of parental dependency that teenagers in our culture experience.

Adolescents and some children frequently go from one extreme to another in testing out their independence and their impact on other people. This is one of the reasons they may dress in what parents think is an outlandish style. If you as a parent should challenge your teenager's taste, and force a confrontation by insisting, for instance, that your teenager dress as you wish, you can be sure that he will rebel and perhaps look even more extreme. In all likelihood it's not what either of you ultimately wants. But if you respect his individuality and give him the freedom he needs, you will probably find that he will make more conservative choices than if you try to impose your values on him.

The problems of dress fads or extreme hairstyles are minor, in comparison to the self-destructive behavior in which some teenagers engage in order to be considered acceptable by their peers. I'm referring to excessive drinking or drug use. You can't police your teenagers all the time, nor can you prevent them from making mistakes. You can be sure, however, that if you establish rigid rules and restrictive limits, your teenagers will become more resentful and perhaps downright defiant. Many parents might disagree with me, believing that unless you severely punish teenagers for violating rules you are condoning unacceptable behavior. But my experience tells me that severe punishments or rigid rules not only provoke even more rebelliousness, but that young people frequently retaliate by developing a negative and self-defeating attitude toward all rules and regulations that come up later in their lives.

What you can *do* is acknowledge your teenagers' independence. Let them know you respect their individuality, but that you have feelings about what they are doing and you want them to know how you feel. If, in the early years, you have had a trusting and close relationship with your child, in all likelihood he will, as an adolescent, be concerned about your feelings and reactions. Despite the defiance and rebelliousness I've seen from teenagers, I'm also aware of the fact that they want parental acceptance and love. If you respect their individuality, in spite of some hazards that may be involved in giving them the freedom they need, there is less chance that they will defy you in self-destructive ways. Stress that it's not easy for parents to simply let children go off on their own without any rules or guidelines. Emphasize that it's not their irresponsibility that upsets or worries you, but rather that in certain situations you are concerned about the possible dangers that could come up.

If your teenager is inclined to continue violating rules, you should let him know that it disappoints you and makes it more difficult for you to allow the freedom you want to give him. Even then, don't take a harsh or punitive position, as this simply will cause him to "dig in" even more firmly. The greater the understanding and acceptance of his individuality on your part, the easier it will be for him to show respect for your feelings and wishes.

REGRESSION
(SEE ALSO *Bedwetting, Breastfeeding, Death, Divorce, Hospitalization, Illness, Moving, Sibling, Toilet Training, Weaning*)

It is not unusual for young children to revert to "immature" or babylike behavior when they are under some sort of stress—from the arrival of a new baby or the death of a relative, from moving to a new place, or parents' divorce. Regressive behavior usually takes the form of a weaned child's wanting to return to the bottle or breast, or a toilet-trained child's wetting or having bowel movements in his pants or wetting his bed at night more frequently. Some children adopt a babylike speech pattern or whine a great deal.

Whatever the reason, the regression to sometimes infantile behavior is usually brief and, with parental understanding, can be alleviated. Let's take the example of a new baby in the household. For a period following the arrival of a new sibling, a parent may find that an older child will show some regressive behavior. By being "just like the baby," the older child may feel that he will gain the same care and attention. But after he has adjusted to the birth and realizes that he is still loved and respected, he will usually give up these temporarily acquired infantile behavior patterns. If you spend more time with him alone on occasions when he doesn't necessarily demand it or crave it, and in a way that you know he enjoys, it will help overcome regressive behavior. In this way you will be satisfying his need to know that he is still worthy of your love, even though he is not a new baby.

REJECTION
(SEE ALSO *Acceptance, Babysitter, Child Abuse, Death, Divorce, Rebellion, Sibling*)

Some children are indeed clearly rejected—severe punishments, rigid limits, and neglect convince a child of this. However, throughout infancy and childhood, most children will at one time or another feel rejected by their parents, and most of the time this feeling is not based on fact. The parents may simply have gone out for an evening and left the young child with an unfamiliar babysitter. When a new sibling arrives on the scene the older child is bound to feel rejected, seeing how much time and attention is being devoted to the baby. When parents separate or divorce, the child may feel rejected by the parent who leaves. When a parent dies, the child will feel abandoned—and rejected—by that parent.

Sometimes children feel rejected for somewhat more subtle reasons—even though their parents insist that of course they love their children and have given them "every advantage." If parents provide for their children's physical well-being, and yet frequently leave them, make little effort to do things with them, show little interest in their activities, give them little praise or approval, it should not be surprising that the child feels rejected despite the parents' disclaimer. If a parent sees a child as a burden or a disappointment, the child will sense this and rightfully feel rejected.

Feelings of rejection can be avoided if you encourage and praise your child, show your child that you love and care about him, and are interested in those thoughts, feelings, and activities he wants to share with you. If your child has deep feelings of rejection and resentment, however, it may be necessary to seek professional psychological help—for the whole family.

RELIGION
(SEE ALSO *Adolescence, Independence, Individuality, Rebellion*)

If there is one topic that can be both a source of comfort and contention in a family, it is religious belief. Children have complained to me that they are being forced to comply, against their will, to their parents' religion. These youngsters, most often adolescents, feel rebellious and resentful about being coerced into attending services or afterschool religious instruction when they "don't believe that stuff anymore." Their parents often despair that these children will not follow in the family faith and tradition.

I can understand the consternation of parents with children defying their religion, but I must tell you that the harder a parent pushes on this issue, the more adamant a child will be. Many young people, when trying to assert their independence and establish their individuality, find it difficult to be self-reliant without rebelling against the very people on whom they have been dependent. This means that frequently they reject their parents' religious beliefs in order to assert themselves.

There is no way you can force your child to accept your religious beliefs. In fact, a strong or punitive stand will likely increase her resistance. If, on the other hand, you show respect for your child's feelings, you can rightfully ask that she show the same consideration for yours. Let her know you feel strongly about this but you have no intention of forcing her to accept your beliefs. If you allow your child to work things out in her own way, you leave open the option for her to come around to your beliefs at another time.

I should point out that the child who feels she gains emotional security and respect from her parents will likely remain an active member of that family in spite of differences of religious opinion. She will return to celebrate in family festivities, many of which coincide with religious holidays.

Some parents still feel distraught over a child's refusal to attend religious school. I think the first thing to do is to determine exactly why the child does not want to go. Some children find religious or Sunday school too harsh (a particular teacher may be overbearing or punitive) or restrictive (the child may be overworked with afterschool activities). Whatever the reason, it is important that you discuss it.

I don't think that there is much to be gained by insisting that a child attend Sunday school; it may turn her off completely to religion. But I think you can fairly ask your child to at least try Sunday school for a short time. If you take such a compromising attitude, your child may find it rewarding or interesting enough to continue on her own.

So far I've discussed the problems that can arise for parents with firm religious beliefs. But unreligious parents have also asked me whether they should provide their children with religious instruction. I don't think it's wise to pretend, for your child's sake, that you have religious beliefs. Children are usually sensitive enough to recognize when someone is being insincere.

All things being equal, there is no evidence to suggest that children who do not have a religious background suffer in terms of their emotional adjustment, or that their moral judgment is impaired. Conducting yourself in an ethical manner and developing a strong value system depends more on your whole experience as a child rather than the presence or absence of religion. Usually, by the time they are adolescents, children will be seeking their own answers to a great many questions, including religious questions.

RESPONSIBILITY
(SEE ALSO *Allowance, Family, Laziness, Sibling*)

I believe that it is important for everyone in a family to cooperate in handling family responsibilities and to share in the work as well as the pleasures of family life. This gives children a sense of their own capabilities as well as a feeling of importance within the family unit.

A parent who teaches a sense of responsible and loving concern for others makes an invaluable imprint on a young personality. The satisfaction it can give your child when he helps you, a brother or sister, or a friend or neighbor is one of life's greatest rewards. And of course from a practical standpoint, many homes could not function comfortably without the care and assistance of the children.

Certainly, older siblings can and should be expected to help out with younger ones. But to make sure that this is a positive experience for everyone involved, it is up to parents to conscientiously evaluate each situation. A key factor is the parents' attitude. Parents are sometimes quick to *demand* that an older child care for a younger sibling simply as an obligation; in doing so, they show little positive recognition of what the older child has done. This can lead to resentment and a resistance to sharing family responsibilities. By openly discussing with your children your reasons for needing their help, and by showing your pride and gratitude for their efforts, you will give your children a feeling of self-esteem.

It is also important to remember that children have a right to live their own lives, and that while family responsibilities are important, they should not be so great that they severely limit the older children's participation in activities with their peers. Being constantly burdened with caring for a little brother or sister, while all the other children are socializing or playing without such encumbrances, can understandably cause resentment toward parents and toward the little ones.

As far as other general guidelines are concerned, it is best to avoid having one child assume responsibility for another child who is close in age—say, less than three or four years apart. Such children are likely to be at similar stages of development, and are not separated by a time span that makes one clearly more knowledgeable or reliable than the other.

The personalities and characteristics of all the children involved are also important. Remember that in the long run, leaving immature or squabbling children together may cause more problems than it will ever solve.

In my experience, the more positive recognition that parents show toward older siblings who assume any of these responsibilities, the more the youngsters will take these responsibilities upon themselves. Ultimately they will need little or no prompting to help out. Some children I know take over quite spontaneously in helping younger siblings with homework; some pass on such skills as riding a bike; some even give advice on all sorts of problems and concerns.

My own son, Eric, has always volunteered to do things with his sister, Pia, who is six years younger. I have always been delighted by his sensitivity to his sister and have been particularly pleased at the way in which he marveled at her paintings and unhesitatingly helped her with some of her school science projects. I am sure the pride I have expressed in his warmth and patience with his sister have helped make this a positive experience for him—and the love that radiates from Pia to her brother indicates that she feels the same way. Pia, in turn, has picked up Eric's interest in younger children. She begs me to invite to dinner people who have babies so that she can take care of the babies while their parents are eating.

I do not believe that children should be paid for individual chores within the family. In my opinion, a child who is paid for completing individual tasks will not develop a feeling that his efforts are an important part of the effort that is necessary for all family members to contribute.

Sharing responsibilities within a family leads to a greater sense of self-esteem for all, reinforces family ties, and provides children with a positive model regarding human life. I believe the greatest satisfactions human beings can gain in life are those that involve the sharing of life's burdens and pleasures alike, and the deep sense of fulfillment that results.

RESTAURANTS

Many parents wonder whether it is advisable to take infants to restaurants. To be sure, there are many restaurants that will do everything in their power to make it clear that they dislike children (from saying so to keeping you waiting endlessly for the least desirable tables). But I see no reason why your young child should not be taken to a restaurant.

Having your baby along may force you to put aside your meal long enough to tend to his needs from time to time, but nothing in the process harms your baby. And from a practical point of view, taking a baby to a restaurant enables you to get out once in a while without having to pay for a babysitter. Obviously, you would want to steer clear of very formal places, where the emphasis is on anything but the needs of babies.

One word of caution: If you take your baby out at night, prepare yourself for some disapproving soul telling you that you are interfering with your baby's need for sleep, or that "Night air is bad for your child." There is no basis whatsoever for this advice. In fact, at nighttime all air is "night air," whether you're at home or not.

RETARDATION

(SEE ALSO *Handicapped or Chronically Ill Child, Intelligence Quotient, Language Development Problems, Neurological Disturbances*)

Slow development does not necessarily mean that a child is mentally retarded. Each child has some unique qualities in his growth pattern. Some children walk at a later age than most, but speak earlier. As long as your child reaches each of the milestones of development—lifting the head, reaching for objects, responding to facial expressions, sitting up, standing, walking, and talking—more or less within the average time period, there is little to be concerned about. However, if he shows definite slowness in a number of these skills, then special help should be sought from a pediatric psychologist.

If you find that your child does in fact have a clearly diagnosed retardation of one sort or another, there are support groups and special organizations that are available to provide help. These can be located through your pediatrician or a local medical center.

If you have other children, I think that you should be open with them in discussing the abilities and limitations of their retarded sibling. Not dealing with the issue can only confuse or even upset your children. They may construe your silence as shame. Explain the situation as best you can, and ask for help in dealing with it. Emphasize that you will always be available to answer any questions that might come up, or to help solve any problems.

You may find yourself giving a great deal of attention to your retarded child, if only because he seems to require more. Your other children may occasionally express their anger at feeling left out by teasing their retarded sibling.

It is entirely appropriate for you to offer special attention to your retarded child, but it is also understandable that your other children may feel neglected. You can then give each of your children your undivided attention at times when they don't demand it but would certainly like it. If you are only attentive after your children protest, they will learn to protest frequently. But if, instead, you make a real attempt to provide the attention that all your children need, they will be more content and their relationships with their retarded sibling and with you should improve.

As difficult as it may be to raise a child who has a special problem such as retardation, it is my view that families with a retarded or otherwise handicapped child may gain a greater sense of solidarity, a greater respect for the individuality of each person, and a greater compassion for those who experience hardships than do other families.

REWARDS
(SEE ALSO *Allowance, Behavior Modification, Discipline and Punishment, Praise, Responsibility*)

Rewarding a child with recognition and pride for acceptable behavior, good grades, or a job well done is a positive parental act. We all need recognition for accomplishments, and this can be an incentive for deeds yet to be achieved. Material goods never accomplish the same satisfaction.

When parents use material rewards or bribes in place of approval and encouragement, they create a connection between acceptable behavior and an object that represents acceptance and love. The child who is invariably bribed or rewarded with presents develops a desire to acquire material things. Often, a child who is rewarded with objects (or punished by having his possessions taken away) associates these things with love. In effect, he comes to believe that possessing an object is the equivalent of having love.

A child who is raised this way demands rewards for achievement and may show little motivation—at school, for example—unless his parents promise to give him some *thing* as a trophy. Many times I have been consulted by parents of college students who are upset because their children lack motivation and refuse to study unless they are "bribed" with the promise of a new car for achieving certain grades. These children find it difficult to gain any inherent joy out of what they do since they gauge their achievements only in terms of the material things that can be acquired by their efforts.

When a child makes this association, he may constantly need to acquire things as an adult, looking for some fulfillment through adding to his possessions.

It is important to remember that using acceptance and affection as a reward is, in the long run, much more fulfilling and emotionally healthy than offering material rewards as an incentive for acceptable behavior. These feelings help a child develop sensitivity to others, and to find learning or working rewarding because it provides self-esteem through recognition from people they respect. Parental attention and signs of approval are extremely important and go a long way toward motivating a child to succeed in life.

S

SANTA CLAUS

I'm not opposed to the myth of Santa Claus. Actually, that's just what I favor. A *myth* is a story passed down from generation to generation, or as Webster's dictionary puts it, "a person or thing existing only in imagination." I'm not opposed to the myth; I'm opposed to telling children that Santa Claus is real.

While I don't recommend stopping youngsters as they walk down the street and telling them that "Santa Claus is a fake," I do believe that children should be told the truth about Santa Claus when they ask if he is real. I believe it is best to tell children that Santa Claus is a make-believe person and that both children and grown-ups pretend that he brings presents at Christmas time. Children are delighted that adults can engage in make-believe too, and they are capable of enjoying such fantasies, sometimes finding them even more satisfying than reality.

Saying Santa Claus is real requires many lies. How do you explain all the Santas in all the different stores at Christmas time? How does he get down the chimney when you don't have a fireplace? And most importantly, how do you one day explain that all the answers you gave to all these questions weren't really true? I think it's crucially important for parents to be honest with their children. If you lead them to believe that Santa Claus is real they may later doubt your credibility as a parent.

SCHIZOPHRENIA
(SEE ALSO *Autism, Crying, Infancy, Withdrawn Child*)

I want to emphasize at the outset that this is a mental disease that can *only* be diagnosed by a licensed, certified psychologist or psychiatrist. If your child exhibits some or even all of the symptoms typical of schizophrenics, it *does not* mean he has this mental illness.

Because of popular accounts of mental illness, people often believe a schizophrenic has a "split personality." This is not necessarily so. More commonly, a schizophrenic is withdrawn from the world. He will sit for hours without any apparent interest in his surroundings, and has basically lost touch with reality. He cannot separate what is real from what is fantasy. Schizophrenics sometimes have hallucinations—they see, hear, or feel things that are not there. Normal people sometimes think they have seen or heard something but know it did not really happen. Schizophrenics not only experience something that is not there, but react to it as if it were real.

It is rare for pre-teenagers to exhibit such behavior, but very young children and infants can be withdrawn. I have seen this in babies who have been left to "cry it out." The baby whose cries are ignored eventually tunes out the world and turns inward. He develops this mechanism of withdrawal from reality and will use it whenever he is faced with stress. He may show no eye contact with others, no preference for people over objects, and may engage in excessive self-stimulation. While this baby may not be a schizophrenic, he has, in fact, developed a defense mechanism characteristic of schizophrenics—a pattern he could carry with him into adult life.

No one knows for certain the causes of schizophrenia, but some researchers believe it is biochemical in origin, and hereditary. Some children who are seemingly normal may suddenly behave like a schizophrenic, triggered by a traumatic event or emotional shock. People born with a predisposition to schizophrenia may be able to avoid it, some psychologists and psychiatrists believe, if they receive a lot of parental love and attention.

This may seem like a bleak picture, and indeed, the outlook for most schizophrenics is not good. About a quarter of the children suffering from schizophrenia seem to improve greatly with psychotherapy and calming drugs. They can adjust to later social life. However, the bulk of schizophrenics require treatment and care the rest of their lives. Constant research in this field does offer some hope for the future.

SCHOOL
(SEE ALSO *Fears, Gifted Child, Homework, Hyperactivity, Independence, Intelligence Quotient, Learning, Sex Education, Teacher*)

Most children are ready to begin school around the age of three when they are weaned, toilet trained, and independent enough to be able to spend time away from their parents. Putting your child in school before this age is not advisable since younger children are usually not capable of interacting in a meaningful way. They engage in what is described as "parallel play"—that is, playing alongside each other instead of with each other.

Most three-year-olds who attend nursery school and five-year-olds who go to kindergarten are eager to begin school. You won't need to induce your child's interest so much as reduce any anxiety he may feel. When you prepare your child for school, stick to the facts about what will happen there. Explain in concrete terms when he will go, what he will do there, and when you will pick him up. This will give him a clearer view of what to expect than if you just say "It will be lots of fun and there will be lots of nice children there." You might also let him know that at first he may be unhappy and lonely, but that he will eventually get used to school. You can explain that some children might even cry when their mommies leave. I think it is far better to give your child a realistic idea of what will go on. Otherwise, if you paint a completely rosy picture, and something untoward happens, he might be overwhelmed and disappointed.

There are any number of reasons why a child will act negatively about going to school: if there are younger siblings at home he may feel as though he is being "kicked out of the house"; the teacher may be scary or unresponsive to his needs; sometimes other children in the class will bully or terrorize him. If your child does react

173

negatively, I suggest that you stay in school with him. Some youngsters simply need a longer period of time to adjust to school and are less ready to be separated from their parents, whom they can count on for security.

Another common reason for a child's reluctance to attend school, even after his initial adjustment, is that he may be unable to perform at the level expected of him. This inability can lead to a sense of failure. If your child is doing poorly in school, he may have a learning disability associated with some minor neurological dysfunction or some glandular disturbance. Such problems usually begin in the first or second grade.

Some children try to feign illness in order to avoid school. The most important thing to do is try to uncover the reason for his reluctance.

If your child is doing poorly in school, of course you should speak to his teacher. It is conceivable that your child needs tutorial help or is in a class where the other pupils are extremely competitive; your child may feel left out unless he can achieve at a higher level. In order to keep your child's motivation from flagging, assure him that you are proud of his efforts. Make it clear that it is not essential for people to be the best in everything but that you consider it important for a person to try hard. Let him know you understand that he is doing this and that you admire him for it. Under no circumstances should you criticize or belittle a child for the report card he brings home. You may express concern and a willingness to help him improve, but critical remarks will make your child feel rejected and resentful.

SEPARATION ANXIETY
(SEE ALSO *Babysitter, Day Care, Fears, Independence, Neurosis, Sleep, Summer Camp, Travel*)

Abandonment is often a child's worst fear. All children are afraid of losing the adults who are closest to them and on whom they depend for the greatest amount of love and emotional support. Consequently we see separation anxiety in all children.

An intense and unremitting anxiety may be due to frightening experiences perpetrated by well-meaning adults. For instance, a parent with all good intentions may put a child to sleep, have a strange babysitter come to the house, and then go off to a movie. The child awakens, sees an unfamiliar person, and feels panic. One experience like this and a child becomes desperate to have a parent near at all times.

I think it is important to introduce babysitters gradually during the first year of a child's life so that she realizes that other people can care for her adequately when her parents are not around. However, make sure that your child knows that you are leaving, reassure her that you will return, and try not to make the initial separations longer than a few hours. It is best if you maintain the same few familiar people as babysitters.

If your child cannot be separated from you without crying indefinitely, you may need to seek professional help to gain insight into your specific situation. Often, though, children get over the problem spontaneously if their parents do not try to fool the child while they sneak away, or make false promises of gifts or events that might occur if the child will let them go.

Going away to camp, or for overnight visits with family or friends, can also make a child anxious about separation. It is quite common for children to become enthusiastic about a visit before it actually takes place. It represents "growing up" and "independence," and in their fantasies everything goes well. But occasionally, things might look different in reality and a child can feel frightened. The camp might be bigger then expected, the activities less to the child's liking, and the other children not nearly as friendly. The child may feel lonely, and overwhelmed. I would say that children under age ten or eleven still need a great deal of parental protection and help in dealing with the things they fear. If your young child can't "stick it out" on a solo visit away from home, you should go to her and reassure her that she tried, and even though it didn't work out this time, perhaps it will the next time. In this way you show recognition of her fears and respect for her feelings, and avoid having her see this experience as a failure.

As a general rule, when parents prepare children for separations such as this, it is wise to let them know in advance that it may not work out and that they may feel homesick.

If you approach a situation like this with understanding, your child is likely to tell you what it is that caused her fear to become so intense that she had to come home. If you have this kind of relationship with your child and she feels capable of expressing her feelings, you can help her more effectively in dealing with her separation anxiety than if you tease her, make fun of her, or make her feel like a failure. Let her know you will give her all the support she needs the next time she plans a visit away, and perhaps you can make it a shorter visit and less challenging.

SEX EDUCATION
(SEE ALSO *Childbirth, Sexual Experiences*)

While I am in favor of schools offering instruction about sex, I don't recommend that you wait until your child is in school to tell her the facts of life. Most children begin asking questions about reproduction—though not about sex—at a very early age—two, three, four at the very latest. Often these questions are precipitated by the impending arrival of a new sibling, and the child initially asks quite simply and directly, "Where did I come from?" or "Where do babies come from?"

When these first questions come up I think you should answer them in a simple and matter-of-fact way. What you tell your child will depend on her age, but I would say that the general rule is to give her only information that she will understand. Your answer should satisfy your child's curiosity about sex, which in all likelihood is on a par with the same innocence and curiosity about rockets going into space. It helps a great deal to have books with diagrams of a man's and woman's body and also a pregnant woman's body to show the place you talk about. I cannot tell you exactly how you should deal with your own child, but I think the average youngster can understand this:

A baby grows from an egg inside a woman. The egg is very tiny, about the size of the head of a pin. A woman grows many eggs inside her in a place called an ovary. They don't all grow at once.

A baby starts to grow when a sperm from inside a man comes together with a very tiny egg inside a woman's body. It takes about nine months for that tiny egg to grow into a full-sized baby, and this happens inside the woman's body in a place called the uterus, which is near the stomach (don't say it *is* the stomach). As the baby gets larger and larger, the woman's body gets bigger and bigger in the place where the baby is growing. When the baby is ready to be born, the woman usually goes to the hospital and has the help of a doctor or a midwife to help the baby be born.

A child will probably ask, "How does the baby get out?" You can explain by saying, "Most babies are born through the vagina, which gets bigger when the baby is ready to be born, and then afterward gets smaller again." It's not necessary to go into detail about caesarian section unless the child asks specifically about it or unless it's personally relevant—if, for example, one of your children was born by caesarian section.

The question most parents find most difficult is, "How does the sperm get from the man's body into the woman's body?" You need not wait for a child to ask this—in fact, it might be best to show a willingness to offer this information. You might ask the child, "Wouldn't you like to know how it happens?" If the child seems interested, you might say something like this:

When a man and a women love each other a lot, they enjoy hugging and kissing and being close to each other. This gives them a warm and loving feeling and makes them want to get as close as possible to each other. Sometimes both of them want the man's penis to go into the woman's vagina. This usually makes them both feel very good, and often, as they move around together, sperm comes through the man's penis and out into where the egg is in the woman's body. When one tiny sperm becomes connected to the tiny egg, the baby starts to grow.

You can expect that your child may ask, "The next time Daddy plants a seed in your vagina, can I watch?" Just explain that this is something people like to do when they are alone. It is very special and private.

I realize that many parents are apprehensive about giving this type of information, for fear that their child will tell all the other children in the neighborhood. If this is the case you can tell your child that not all parents believe in telling children these things, and that it might be best if your child did not explain this to her friends, but let her friends' parents tell them.

I feel quite strongly that children's questions about reproduction should be answered honestly and directly. Otherwise, they may pick up misinformation, or feel confused or worried or even frightened. I also think you should avoid potential confusion for your children by using language that is straightforward. The words penis and vagina, for instance, have no negative connotations, and there is no reason not to use them.

As your children get older, I think you should discuss the physical and emotional changes that will take place as they approach their teenage years. If children know about menstruation or wet dreams, they are far less likely to be disconcerted or frightened by these experiences.

Although it is generally assumed that fathers should talk to sons and mothers to daughters, I don't agree that this should necessarily be so. In my opinion, it's far better if parents can feel free to discuss sexual matters with their children regardless of their gender.

Find a time when everyone is in a good mood, and bring the matter up casually—whether your children have done so or not. You might explain that as boys mature, semen—a white, sticky substance that has sperm in it—is stored in their testicles. When they have sexual dreams that are exciting, it can cause the semen to come out in their sleep. This is a normal part of growing up that most people refer to as a "wet dream." In the same way, you can say that when a girl reaches the time at which she can begin to have babies, once a month an egg goes from her ovary into her uterus. If it is not fertilized, the egg leaves her body through her vagina, and a little bit of blood comes with it. This is called menstruation. It lasts for a few days every month, and most people refer to it as a "menstrual period."

As children approach the teenage years, many parents wonder whether they should bring up the subject of birth control and the responsibilities of intercourse. Often, parents worry that by discussing this they will be implicitly condoning sexual activity among teenagers, or will even be putting ideas in their teenager's heads.

Parents who avoid the issues in order to "protect" their children are doing them a disservice. It is obvious that teenagers have many opportunities for sexual activity. And after all, parents can refuse to teach their children how to cross busy thoroughfares, but that doesn't prevent the children from venturing out on their own one day—and perhaps getting hit by a car. Our country's birth rate has dropped for women in all age groups except for teenagers, and many experts believe that a lack of basic sex education accounts for this. In my experience, young people who receive information and guidance from parents, whom they trust, are far less likely to get into sexual difficulty than young people whose parents failed to become involved in the transmission of sex education. By displaying a sense of knowledgeable concern, parents provide a model of what responsibility really is.

A discussion of these matters is not as difficult as many parents might think. You can simply and frankly convey to your children the emotional implications and possible consequences of sexual activity. Explain to them that when two people have sexual relations, deep and intense feelings are often involved. Let them know how important it is, in situations where intercourse might possibly occur, to be sensitive to the other person's feelings and to respect the other person's wishes—but at the same time to stand up for his or her own feelings of what is right or what his or her own wishes are. Explain that if pregnancy should occur—and this will be entirely possible if appropriate precautions are not taken—it will mean dealing with an even greater complexity of feelings and responsibilities, at a time in their lives when they should be free to grow and explore a variety of possibilities for their own future.

Let your teenagers know that you will always be available to talk with them about anything that concerns them on this—or any— subject, and that if specific situations arise in which they think it would be helpful to know more about birth-control procedures, you will discuss this with them. Make it clear that while you feel it's important to inform them about birth control and sexual responsibility, you are not suggesting that you think it's advisable for them to become sexually active at present, but that you believe it would be helpful for them to begin to be aware of these matters at this time in their lives.

SEXUAL EXPERIENCES
(SEE ALSO *Adolescence, Homosexuality, Incest, Masturbation, Pornography, Sex Education*)

In a child's life his sexual experiences can range from inadvertent genital stimulation to masturbation to exposure to sexual deviates to adolescent sex. If you understand these different types of sexual experiences, you can better help your child cope with them, should that be necessary.

Usually, sometime during a child's third year sensations in his or her genitals become pleasant. While a child can be sexually aroused even earlier, the experience is usually unintentional. A little boy may have an erection if he is stimulated while his parent is changing his diaper, or a little girl may show pelvic thrusts if her clitoris is stimulated on a rocking horse or bouncing knee. These are normal responses that occur automatically during accidental stimulation. The more sophisticated sexual sensations that occur during the third year are related to masturbation. Children may straddle an object and slide up and down, or place a soft object between their thighs. Stimulating the genitals when they are preoccupied with watching TV or listening to a story is not uncommon. Usually, masturbation decreases when children are between seven and twelve years old, and increases again during adolescence.

There are other sexual experiences in which a child will engage with other children. Playing "doctor" is one of them. Almost every child who has visited a doctor seems to associate this experience with satisfying some degree of sexual curiosity. Children will examine each other's genitals; the usual procedure is to take pants down and look at bottoms. Sometimes children play, "I'll show you mine if you show me yours."

But playing doctor is not the only sexual exploration. Other forms occur as well. For instance, children can play sexually with members of the same sex or members of the opposite sex. Sometimes the game leads to mutual masturbation. Although this is normal behavior, I believe you should let your children know that you are aware of these activities. React as you would with excessive masturbation. That is, don't take a punitive attitude, or threaten your child's self-esteem, or attempt to instill guilt. But don't ignore the activities, either. Suggest that they play something else. But don't be surprised if your children continue their sexual games. After all, sexual activity is very pleasant.

Many parents worry that their children may come into contact with sexual deviates. You can inform and warn your child about sexual deviates without alarming him. You can say that there are some people who feel differently about sex, and that some of these people are "not healthy." In describing such people it is helpful to say that they were not born that way, but became that way because of some bad experience in their lives.

Don't terrorize your child about the possibility of an encounter with a disturbed person, or you may end up with a child who is too fearful to walk to school. However, you can indicate the kinds of things that abnormal people do, such as showing their genitals to other people or trying to touch the bodies of children. Tell your child that children should always tell their parents if someone behaves toward them in that way, that no matter what anyone else says, children should never keep these things secret.

If your child *is* molested or bothered by a stranger, you should give as much support, reassurance, and acceptance as you can. Provide your child every chance to talk about the experience, especially when he is most upset. You can tell him that he has had a very unusual experience, not one that he need fear will be repeated again and again throughout his life. If your child can talk about his experience he will know that he was not responsible for it and is not blamed for it. This is important, because a child who has had such an experience is often afraid his parents will think he somehow initiated it or failed to resist it sufficiently.

If you have been an "askable" parent, one with whom communication is open, especially where sex is concerned, your pre-teenager or teenager is far less likely to get into sexual difficulty than are young people whose parents have neglected to discuss sex with them. I think sex education becomes particularly important when teenagers begin to have sexual experiences. Parents must accept the fact that today there is a greater openness about premarital sex and contraception. Although many mothers and fathers disapprove, saying, "In my day we didn't do such things," the reality is that times have changed tremendously. Teenagers *are* going to engage in sexual activity, and it is the parents' responsibility to educate them about it and to prepare them to act responsibly.

By the time a youngster is old enough to have sex, he should already know about reproduction. Now parents will want to convey the emotional implications and the possible consequences of sexual activity. You can let your teenagers know how important it is, in situations where intercourse might occur, to be sensitive to the other person's feelings and wishes, but at the same time to stand up for his or her own feelings and wishes. I believe you should explain that if pregnancy should occur—and this is certainly possible if appropriate precautions aren't taken—it will mean dealing with an even greater responsibility at a time in their lives when they should be free to grow and to explore.

I think you should make it clear that while you believe it is important to inform them about birth control and sexual responsibility, you are not suggesting that they become sexually active, but only that they be aware of these matters at this time in their lives.

SHARING
(SEE ALSO *Sibling*)

When children are under the age of three, they are not capable of understanding the meaning of sharing. At this stage they are normally egocentric—they think the world revolves around them—and more or less selfish. Generally, they don't know how to play cooperatively *with* other children, even though they may play *alongside* them. In playgrounds from coast to coast, two-year-olds can be heard to insist: "Mine!" "No—Mine!" Frequently children under three will grab what they want, and look perplexed if you try to explain why they shouldn't grab something that is not theirs. In some families where the children are very close in age and are therefore interested in one another's possessions, the problem continues as the children get older.

There are some general guidelines for dealing with this that you can adapt to your family situation. First of all, don't try to establish ground rules for solving a problem of sharing while tempers are high. Wait until all is well with your children, and then talk to them about the important issues involved. Tell them that it is important that they be able to share their possessions; that they be able to borrow things from one another, enjoy them, and return them in good condition. Tell them that it is important that they respect one another as well as one another's belongings, and that sharing can be accomplished without arguments or destructiveness. Ask them how *they* believe the problem can be solved. The more your children are involved in establishing rules, the easier it will be for them to follow through.

Once the rules have been formulated that seem agreeable to everyone, you then have to figure out a plan to deal with violations of these rules. Punishment and reparation are necessary if you are to be in a position of rule-enforcement. Again, ask your children's opinions. Possibly you might suggest that if one breaks or loses something that belongs to the other, it may be replaced by funds drawn from a weekly allowance. However, this could mean too heavy a financial burden for any child, so you might want to work out a formula—you pay half the damages when they occur, and the child pays the other half from his allowance. While this might seem like an injustice to you, I believe that it's part of parenthood, and one of those responsibilities that comes with teaching your child how to handle problems.

Incidentally, you can succeed too well in teaching your child to share. I remember one mother who explained sharing so effectively to her three-year-old daughter that the next day she had to follow up and inform her that the family cat probably just wasn't interested in doing her puzzle with her.

SIBLING
(SEE ALSO *Adoption, Handicapped or Chronically Ill Child, Jealousy, Only Child, Regression, Responsibility, Retardation, Sharing, Twins*)

Most parents who have a child and are expecting another are very much aware of the problems of sibling rivalry. They rightly sense that, unless the situation is handled well, it can lead to intense jealousy or regressive behavior on the part of the older child.

I am often asked by parents how they can minimize sibling rivalry. I think we need to bear in mind some of the child's overriding concerns when confronted with the prospect of a new brother or sister: "Will Mommy and Daddy still love me and pay attention to me? Am I still important to them?"

I think reassuring your child begins with preparing him for the new arrival. I would like to say first that it is best if children are spaced at least three years apart. It isn't until a youngster passes through the negativistic second year that he begins to learn how to share and becomes a little less dependent on his parents for full time attention. A one- or two-year-old can feel very threatened by an infant who is now getting the attention *he* used to receive. Also, when a child is age three he can better understand your explanation of what is happening: Why Mommy has to go to the hospital to have the baby, and why the newborn will need some extra time and attention. I think you should be open and direct about your explanation of the new arrival and encourage your child to ask you questions.

I strongly advocate allowing children to visit their mothers in the hospital just after delivery. This allows the youngster to be involved in the festivities and happiness accompanying the birth of a new baby.

Your older child may not be enthusiastic about the younger child. In fact, he may express strong negative feelings. Point out that even though he may not like the new baby now, he may get to like him when he gets to know him better. Explain that he may not hurt the baby. Tell him that it's all right for him to hold the baby when he wants to, but he must come to tell you so you can help him with the new baby. If you restrict him from being near the new baby this could make him resent the newborn even more. It's natural for a child to be apprehensive and ambivalent about a new arrival. After all, this sibling is going to change the family constellation, maybe for the worse. You can reassure your child that he is loved and admired by spending some extra time alone with him.

Parents with only one child may wonder if they are depriving their child of a playmate or the chance to learn how to share. My feeling is that all children will have playmates and the chance to share when they attend nursery school. It is true that when children interact with one another they develop internal controls and a tolerance for frustration that helps them become socialized. But these experiences are not limited to families with brothers and sisters.

If some "only" children seem obnoxious, this is often because their parents tend to overindulge them out of guilt and give them *things* instead of time and attention. Some parents want to avoid frustrating their children at any cost, supposedly in an effort to protect them from psychological trauma. These children find it difficult to deal with frustration later on and often develop the feeling that the world revolves around them. But this can happen to any child, whether he has brothers and sisters or not.

I am often asked about the "middle child syndrome," in which a middle child is caught between an older sibling who received a great deal of parental attention, and a younger sibling who is currently being cuddled and babied. Some middle children seem confused by this position in the family, while others develop a personality that gives them adequate self-esteem. In my experience I have seen many middle children who are more out-going, sometimes "show-offs" and often very clownish. In a way, they have resolved their problem by displaying a sense of humor that amuses both the older and younger siblings. You can probably minimize this behavior by giving your middle child more individual and undivided attention at times when he isn't specifically asking for it.

A latecomer—a child born a considerable time after his siblings —is often greatly indulged by all members of the family, and there is usually little rivalry or jealousy between him and his siblings. As a result, the baby receives a great deal of attention. I have seen many parents of latecomers enjoy their youngest child so much that they want him to stay young forever, and they tend to keep him dependent. I advise against this.

If brothers and sisters argue frequently and intensely it is often a sign that the children feel short-changed, that each feels the others are depriving him or her of parental attention. This may be the case, as well, if siblings "squeal" on one another frequently, acting as "tattle-tales."

These problems can be avoided if parents treat siblings as individuals right from the beginning, making it clear that each one is a different person with different needs. I recommend that parents give each of their children some concentrated attention—perhaps once or twice a week—as if that child were the only one who counted at that time. It's not the *amount* of time that's most important; it's the fact that the time belongs to the particular child and is geared to that child's own interests and concerns. In addition, parents should be especially careful to avoid comparing one child to another. The parent who says, "Amy, look how nicely Jason cleans his room. Why can't you do that?" leads Amy to feel hostile toward Jason for making her seem "unacceptable." This resentment can cause great friction among children. It is even worse when children use these sorts of dynamics to manipulate their parents: The statement, "Mommy, Jeff just made a face," does not mean that you need reprimand Jeff. I think if parents refuse to respond to the child who tells tales on another, this behavior should end.

SLEEP
(SEE ALSO *Babysitter, Fears, Nap, Separation Anxiety*)

Individual children's need for sleep can vary greatly. Research has shown that some children require a great deal of sleep while others can function adequately on very little. Children who need less sleep develop just as well as children who have a greater need.

Every parent knows how difficult it can be to convince a child who is not tired to go to bed. Some parents insist on a fixed bedtime and this can make sleep a time of conflict rather than a time of comfort. My experience has shown that parents who insist on a rigid bedtime for children do so for their own convenience, in order to get the children out of the way. While I am sympathetic toward parents—they certainly need time for themselves—I think putting children to bed before they are ready can cause more problems than it solves.

Practically speaking, most young children will go through a period when they resist going to bed. They may develop bedtime rituals to avoid having to lie down and go to sleep. "Read me one more story," "Let me have one more glass of water," "I have to go to the bathroom," are just some of the excuses parents hear. In order to make bedtime a positive experience all around I would first suggest that you give your child some advance notice so that she can prepare for it. You might say, "You should be getting into bed in 15 minutes." She is less likely to be resistant to this than if you were to say, "All right, go to bed now." Once your child is in bed, you could read her a story, or spend time talking with her after she is tucked in.

There are a variety of reasons why children are reluctant to go to bed, ranging from fear of the dark to fear of abandonment to nightmares. These problems are bound to crop up at different times in childhood.

Fear of the dark is very real to a child—and to many adults as well—and is something that should not be ridiculed or criticized. If you are sympathetic to your child and encourage her to talk about her fear, you can reassure her that you are close by and will not let anything bad happen. Leaving a "night light" on helps, and opening a child's door so she is not in total darkness will also make her feel more secure. The time-worn and age-tested teddy bear or "security blanket" can also help make the transition to sleep easier.

For a very young child, falling asleep is like being separated from her parents. The child may feel that when she drifts off to sleep (losing consciousness) her parents may disappear. This belief may have some basis in fact if parents "sneak out" for an evening after their child falls asleep. When the child wakes to find a babysitter or other stranger there, instead of her parents, she will understandably come to associate going to bed with her parents' going away. It is for this reason that I am totally against parents leaving the house without letting their child know they will be gone and having the babysitter on hand *before* they leave. Obviously you can't explain this to an infant, but you can leave your baby with someone who is familiar and who has interacted with your child in your presence. Such "precautions" will go a long way toward assuring your child's sense of security and encouraging her willingness to go to sleep.

Around three years of age, your child may report having dreams, and some of them might be mildly frightening to her. Nightmares are not unusual in children between two to six years of age or older. The causes of nightmares can vary from deep-seated anxieties to stomach aches. I don't think the occasional bad dream is a cause for alarm. But if nightmares persist, you may want to seek professional help. In the interim you can offer support by going quickly and calmly to your child's bedside to hold her, offering reassurance while you cuddle her. Turn the light on so she is fully awake, and reassure her that while dreams can sometimes be scary, they are not real. Emphasize that she is safe, you are nearby and won't let anything bad happen. Some children will insist on coming back to bed with their parents. As a general rule, young children should not be encouraged to sleep in their parents' bed. It can cause the child to develop a dependency on his parents as well as interfere with adult privacy. Many psychoanalysts are adamantly against children *ever* sleeping with their parents, but I don't think such a hard line is necessary. However, it is best if this does not become a habit. It's best to explain to your child that she has her own bed to sleep in. You can offer the reassurance your child seeks by taking her to her own bed, saying, "I will lie down next to you while you fall asleep, then I'll return to my own bed." While this may cause protests and tears, I think it's far better to help the child learn to cope with the situation herself than to give in and establish a pattern that may be hard to break.

Children who are restless sleepers often tend to be active in the daytime as well. In bed they'll thrash about, tossing and turning, and sometimes even sitting up. I don't think that this sort of behavior *per se* means that there is an emotional problem. If a child's active sleep behavior is indeed due to tension or anxiety, her emotional state will be reflected in other ways as well. You'll notice signs of tension or unhappiness during her daytime activities. If you see such signs, try to find out what's upsetting her, and to diminish whatever is causing this. If you can't help your child yourself, get special help from a psychologist or psychiatrist who deals with children. However, if your child is generally happy, gets along with other children, does well in school and appears well rested after "restless" nights, then in all likelihood her sleep patterns are just a normal extension of her daytime personality.

SMOKING
(SEE ALSO *Alcohol and Drug Abuse Among Teenagers, Drinking*)

The best way you can prevent your children from smoking cigarettes is to avoid smoking them yourself. Parents who are smokers often find themselves in a paradoxical situation. They don't want their children to become smokers. But, at the same time, they can't shake their own habit. Parents should recognize how strongly their behavior can influence their children. Parents who smoke are not only greatly increasing the likelihood that they will suffer from cancer, lung and heart disease; these parents are, by example, endangering their children's future health. In addition, parents who smoke are providing an example of self-destructive behavior that is frightening to children. Children who know about the relationship between smoking and cancer, for example, often beg their parents to stop. Parents who smoke should explain to their children that smoking is an addiction that is easy to prevent by not smoking in the first place; and then those parents should, for their children's sake if not their own, redouble their efforts to stop smoking.

If your teenager tries smoking cigarettes there is, of course, no way for you to stop him from doing so when he is out of sight. You should acknowledge this, but should also let him know how you feel about his smoking—that it upsets you to see him endangering his health in this way. Do avoid being punitive, however. Perhaps it will help you to maintain a sensible perspective if you are able to recall, during your own adolescence, the frantic and futile arm-waving in which you engaged when your mother or father unexpectedly opened your bedroom door to find you and your best friend "sneaking a smoke." This memory might help you to realize that many, if not most, teenagers sample cigarettes for a brief period only.

SMOTHERING PARENT
(SEE ALSO *Fears, Independence, Individuality, Overprotectiveness*)

It's important for a child's emotional growth to have parents who are affectionate and concerned with the events in the child's life. If parents fail to provide affection and care, their children are highly vulnerable to emotional difficulties. However, parental affection and involvement in a child's life can be carried to the point where it has a smothering effect on a child. A parent who always speaks sweetly to his or her child, never expresses annoyance or anger, has every minute of the child's day organized into "meaningful" and "educational" experiences, and who is in constant contact with the child's teacher, following every detail of the child's progress, may inadvertently create problems. This kind of parental involvement prevents a child from having free time, and is also an emotional burden for the child. Parents who burden their children in this way are not only fostering their child's dependency, but are basically dependent upon their own children and are using them to satisfy their own needs.

Children need some free time, and they need the opportunity to make their own decisions, and their own mistakes. Parents who prevent children from doing so are preventing them from learning, in much the same way that parents who prevent any discomfort are preventing their children from learning how to cope with unpleasant situations.

SOILING
(SEE ALSO *Regression, Toilet Training*)

By the age of three, children generally use the toilet for bowel movements. Sometimes, however, a child goes much beyond three years of age without doing so, or has been successfully bowel trained and then regresses. An "accident" at times of stress, such as the birth of a sibling, is understandable. But if a child of three or older soils himself frequently or regularly, parents should consult a pediatrician to determine if there is a physical cause for this problem.

More often than not the sudden onset of what is technically known as "encopresis" and more popularly called "soiling," is a sign that there is an underlying emotional problem. We see severe encopresis in very regressed adult schizophrenics, and we sometimes also see it in children who are troubled. I remember treating one youngster who was admitted to our hospital with this problem. First, the boy was examined and found to be free of any physical abnormality that could cause his soiling. Then we looked for some pattern in his soiling. The pattern was very clear: the boy only soiled in school, never at home. Further, a teacher whom he disliked had required him to repeat a grade, and it was only then that the soiling had begun. This suggested to me that the boy had little at his disposal to express his anger with his teacher, except for this primitive pattern. In working with this boy, I told him that he was probably soiling himself because he was trying to get back at his teacher. I explained that this would cause him more problems than it would her. I also indicated that it would make him seem unpleasant to friends and to others with whom he had contact. I suggested very strongly that he stop it. There was a dramatic change: the boy's soiling stopped immediately once he understood the connection between what he was doing and the anger at his teacher that had caused it.

SPANKING
(SEE ALSO *Conscience, Discipline and Punishment, Lying*)

In Sweden a law prohibits parents from striking their children or punishing them in humiliating ways, such as withholding meals. In my opinion, this legislation speaks well for the humanity of the Swedish people. Actually, no Swedish parents have been put into jail for spanking, and no penalties have been set for violating this law. But the law does make clear the Swedish view that force or the threat of force is a demeaning, destructive, unfair, and inappropriate way for parents to relate to their children. I share this view. I strongly believe that spanking or other physical punishment does not benefit a child, and can be psychologically harmful.

Spanking establishes a pattern in which physical violence is an acceptable means of controlling the behavior of others. It can only set the stage for further violence later in life. It also can create the kind of resentment in children that can lead to defiance, and contribute to the breakdown of the parent-child relationship.

People who advocate spanking claim that it "straightens children out" and "gets them to do what you want." Even if this is true, I believe that this sort of obedience is only a short-term gain. Over the long term the children's feelings of resentment toward authority figures, and the example of violent behavior can only produce hostility and destruction.

Another lesson a child can come away with is "next time be careful and don't get caught." In other words, children learn to behave in devious ways, they learn to lie rather than to face responsibility for wrongdoing if it means being physically harmed.

We want children to develop a conscience—a humane and compassionate concept of right and wrong—rather than a conviction that "might makes right" or a superficial shrewdness about not getting caught. It is through their parents' example that children learn best. If parents themselves are fair and kind and treat people —including their own children—with respect, children will learn to do so. But if parents do things to hurt people, their children will fear them, resent them, hide things from them, and may behave violently toward other children.

Although I do not believe in spanking, I do believe in discipline. I feel that children need guidelines for their behavior, and feel most comfortable when those guidelines are clear, well-defined, and consistently upheld. Parents should emphasize by their manner, tone of voice, and denial of privileges, that certain behavior is not permissible. Parental values and standards of behavior—and the reasons behind them—should be made clear to children, and the rules for their enactment should be consistently maintained.

STEALING
(SEE ALSO *Cheating, Conscience, Juvenile Delinquency, Lying*)

Stealing can represent a very common, but misguided, adventure. Often stealing means simply that your child is conforming to group pressure. In all likelihood such stealing will be an isolated event, and I believe it is wise to assume that this is the case. If you react to an initial episode by labelling your child a crook or by showing continued mistrust for everything he does, you will destroy your child's self-esteem, and will give him the impression that you expect him to continue to misbehave—a prophecy he may fulfill.

However, if your child's stealing is persistent or chronic, it may be related to a serious underlying emotional problem. If your child is stealing persistently, it may help you to deal with the problem if you understand some of the common causes of stealing in children. Just as some children lie without any feeling that it is wrong, some children steal without feeling that it is wrong; they have never developed a sufficiently strong conscience. Other children, who realize that stealing is wrong, continue to do so in order to retaliate against authorities, such as their parents, toward whom they have very angry feelings. Some children steal in the hope that they will get caught, thus upsetting their parents while also leading their parents to give the children the attention they desire. For other children, stealing is a way of acquiring objects that in some indirect way represent "supplies" of love and the kind of sustenance that is unconsciously related to a sense of strength or self-esteem. Such children use the stolen objects as a hedge against "emotional famine." The objects counteract a feeling of emptiness, or loss. If your child's stealing is persistent or chronic, you should seek professional help.

STEPPARENT
(SEE ALSO *Divorce*)

Some children may have difficulty adjusting to a new stepparent after a parent remarries following a divorce or death in the family. You can help your children make the transition by acknowledging that they will need to make it gradually. It is perfectly understandable for them to still have emotional ties to the mother or father with whom they are no longer living or the parent who has died. If you remarry, let your children have the chance to get to know your intended spouse over a period of time so that they can adjust to him or her as your friend. This must come before you can expect them to accept this person as your new spouse.

Some people in the role of new parents tend to be oversolicitous or to overindulge their "new" children in an effort to be liked and accepted. This can be as difficult for the parents as it is for the children. Everyone involved wants to be accepted, but children are likely to test the new family members and look for injustices and inconsistencies.

It is not unusual for a child to say, "You're not my mother, so why should I do what you say?" I think you can best deal with this by responding, "Yes, I know I'm not your mother. I'm your father's new wife, and no one will ever replace your mother. But that doesn't mean I can't set rules in my house." Let the child know you respect her feelings and that you would like her to respect yours. You might point out that teachers are not their students' parents, but they too set rules.

There will undoubtedly be times when you feel as though the children are goading you. Try to understand that as malicious as it may seem, they are trying to test you and find out your strengths and weaknesses. If you lose your temper, or become overly harsh in punishment, you will weaken your position. Try to bear with their complaining, discuss problems as much as you can, and don't be afraid to stand firm on the things you believe in.

I feel that the best way to avoid confusion about discipline is to stand by the rules that you find appropriate in your lifestyle. You can be sure that children will make comparisons between their "new" and "old" families in an effort to find out what the limits are in their "new" family. This is only fair, and helps children to make the adjustment eventually. For example, you will hear, "You're so mean, Mom. When I'm at Dad's house his new wife lets me stay up as late as I want." The best approach to this is to avoid being intimidated, angry, or defensive. Make it clear that whatever happens in the other house with the other parent has nothing to do with what you set up as standards of acceptable behavior in your home.

I know that it may seem difficult at times, but with patience and understanding you can eventually establish a comfortable situation with your new family. Realistically speaking, however, there are some children who may never be able to accept a new parent. Likewise, there are some parents who find it difficult to warm up to a new child. I think professional family counseling is extremely helpful when such apparent incompatibilities persist.

STUBBORNNESS
(SEE ALSO *Defiance, Individuality, Toilet Training*)

A more polite word for stubbornness might be willfullness. A willful person is one who is reluctant to change his mind, listen to reason, or learn from experience. Often, the willful child has willful parents who have in a sense taught him this behavior. Many times this tendency grows out of a child's having been constantly challenged or completely dominated by his parents during the early years of his life, when he was most helpless. Willfullness seems to be related in particular to coercive bowel training and rigid feeding schedules. The child who has been forced to do things regardless of his own will is likely to grow up to become either stubborn or passive. His passivity may take the form of "passive-aggressive" behavior; that is, unlike a defiant person, he does not do the *opposite* of what he is told to do; instead, he simply does not *do* anything that other people might request, however reasonable it may be.

As an example of passive-aggressive behavior I can remember one nine-year-old boy whose mother insisted that he clean his room by noon one Saturday. When the mother inspected the room at noon, the boy had not even begun the job. He'd "forgotten." She again insisted that he begin. He began—at a snail's pace. As soon as she left the room, he stopped working. When she returned an hour later, he'd fallen asleep. He never once came right out and *refused* to clean his room—still, he managed to avoid cleaning his room.

If you want to prevent willfullness in your child, it would be wise to avoid rigidity in feeding and coerciveness in bowel training. You should encourage your child to express his own feelings and to develop his individual wants, needs, abilities, and interests.

STUTTERING
(SEE ALSO *Language Development Problems, Neurological Disturbances*)

I believe that stuttering has a physiological basis. It does seem clear, however, that certain environmental factors, including stress, play some role. For example, stress is often transitory, occurring only when a child is under some sort of pressure or has experienced a frightening event. Also, many children begin to stutter when they start school, which may be a stressful event.

On the positive side, new treatments for stuttering are constantly being designed. In addition, about eighty percent of stutterers outgrow their problem—with or without therapy—by the end of adolescence.

Of course, in the meantime, it is very frustrating for a child when he wants to say something and cannot get it out. It only makes it worse when listeners respond by becoming impatient and anxious, allowing their facial expressions to reflect the stutterer's difficulty and pain, attempting to hurry the stutterer along, and supplying the missing words for the stutterer.

There is no way to force a child to stop stuttering. Punishment and ridicule exacerbate it. If your child stutters, the best way for you to deal with it is to be extremely patient and avoid getting upset yourself. You should try to eliminate whatever stressful situations your child is involved in. You should give your child the opportunity to express all his feelings—even those that are negative—reassuring him that you accept and love him no matter what.

If stuttering persists, it may be necessary to look for some underlying emotional problem. Generally speaking, a child's inability to communicate represents a fear that he will say something unacceptable that might make his parents reject him. If your child has repressed hostile and aggressive feelings, and fears that they may come to the surface, stuttering may be the result. If despite your efforts, your child continues to stutter, you would do well to consult your pediatrician, who may recommend that your child see a speech pathologist specializing in stuttering therapy, or a psychotherapist.

SUCKING
(SEE ALSO *Breastfeeding, Infancy, Instincts, Pacifier, Thumbsucking, Weaning*)

A newborn initially establishes contact with the world through his mouth and the sucking reflex. Since an infant begins sucking almost as soon as an object is placed in his mouth, we can assume that the sucking response in instinctual. There is even evidence that the sucking exists before birth. Photographs have shown fetuses thumbsucking, and some babies are born with callouses on the thumb, indicating sucking before birth.

The sucking reflex facilitates contact with the nipple from which infants receive food. Finding the nipple is accomplished with another natural reflex that occurs at the same time as the sucking reflex. If you touch your baby's face somewhere near his mouth he will move in the direction of the touch. This is known as the rooting response. Combined with sucking, this rudimentary behavior pattern leads a child to a source of food and thus helps provide sufficient nutrition for survival.

SUFFERING
(SEE ALSO *Death, Doctor/Medical Examination, Handicapped or Chronically Ill Child, Hospitalization, Illness, Teething, Terminal Illness*)

Some doctors believe that when a child is in extreme pain that cannot be relieved, or has to undergo a painful medical procedure, the parents should leave that child alone. After all, they argue, nothing can be done and the child will associate the pain with the adult present, and therefore resent the parent. I could not disagree more with this notion. In my years of working with hospitalized children I have found that in such circumstances the relations between parents and children become stronger and better when the parent is there to offer comfort and support. Even an infant is able to *feel* the compassion of a parent trying to comfort him. Even though you cannot take away the hurt, your child knows that you are trying. As difficult as it may be for you to see your child so upset, holding him, cuddling him, and being with him during his pain will convince your child of your love. Far from resenting you, he will learn to trust you even more. I've known of children who have been hospitalized and have seemed to be sleeping as their parents sat in the same room with them hour after hour. The parents sometimes wondered whether their presence did their child any good until the child sleepily asked, "Are you there, Mom and Dad?" and when the parents answered in the affirmative, the child said, "Good," smiled, and went back to sleep. The parents then had no doubt that their child knew and was glad that they were with him even if he was in pain.

SUICIDE
(SEE ALSO *Alcohol and Drug Abuse Among Teenagers, Depression*)

Tens of thousands of teenagers attempt suicide each year in the United States. Studies of this tragic phenomenon have concluded that adolescent suicides stem primarily from family problems. Simply, self-destructive teenagers failed, for one reason or another, to get the love and nurturing they needed in order to feel that life was worth living.

There are a number of clues parents can watch for in adolescents. Some of these clues—notably a previous suicide attempt, threats of suicide, or talk about suicide—are fairly obvious. However, studies have found that the teenagers who were the greatest suicide risks were not only the rebellious, defiant ones who got into trouble frequently, but also the withdrawn, friendless "loners," and those who experienced a sudden trauma.

If you see the signs of a suicide attempt in your teenager, or in a teenager who is close to you, by all means make every effort to get psychological help for the youngster as soon as possible.

SUMMER CAMP
(SEE ALSO *Fears, Independence, Separation Anxiety*)

Summer camp can be a valuable experience for many children. If your child expresses an interest in going to camp, you can discuss this as a family, going over the brochures that describe various camps, and talking about the pros and cons of each possibility. Sometimes camp directors or representatives will come to your home to show slides and answer questions about the camp. You and your child can also talk with those of your child's friends who have gone to camp.

You should prepare your child for the possibility that he may feel homesick, especially during the first few days. You can add that most children get over it, and many can't wait to return the next year.

If your child calls you from camp, sobbing and begging to come home, it is important for you to recognize his fears and respect his feelings. If you approach the situation with understanding, and your child feels free to express his feelings, he is more likely to calm down and eventually come around to telling you exactly what has caused him to have such an intense reaction that he would like to come home. Perhaps he will even get to the point where he says he would *prefer* to stick it out, and then it might be possible for you to encourage him to do so. It might be helpful for you to talk with your child's counselor or the camp director, as well.

Whether you allow your child to come home, suggest that he think about it for a few days, or tell him that you understand how unhappy he is but that he has made a commitment that you strongly urge him to keep, depends on you, your child—especially his age and relative maturity—and the particular circumstances. But you should definitely listen carefully to your child, and indicate that you respect his feelings and ideas, and understand what he is going through. It can never be helpful—only harmful—for you to tease him, make fun of him, or make him feel like a failure.

If your child does not want to go to camp in the first place, it would be wise not to insist that he do so. Some children simply prefer more family-oriented situations. If you force your child to go to camp, you could make him resentful, and could also create so much separation anxiety that it would interfere with his developing independence. Let his independence emerge with encouragement—

he can start with overnight visits to friends or relatives, if he likes —but don't insist that he take a long stint away from home until he feels ready.

You might find it helpful if your whole family visits a summer camp, to get a more realistic idea of what's there. Perhaps in the course of the family's summer vacation you can plan such a trip. But do give your child the option of deciding on his own whether this is what he wants next year.

T

TEACHER
(SEE ALSO *Learning, School*)

It is a fact of life that some teachers—just like some parents—are better than others. It would be wonderful if your child had the best possible teacher every year he went to school, but it would hardly be likely. Besides differences in teaching skill as such, there are personality characteristics that make different teachers respond differently to different students.

If your child complains about his teacher, I think you should listen carefully to him, and allow him to express his feelings about this situation. Perhaps you might talk to the teacher to get another perspective on the problem. But do not be critical of your child's teacher. If you are, you will undermine the teacher's position and contribute to your child's lack of motivation. You can simply acknowledge that yes, this teacher is different from last year's teacher. You can then explain that not all teachers are the same, that some are more friendly, or more interesting, or more interested in particular students, than others. Point out to your child that throughout life he will have to deal with people who are not necessarily appealing to him.

Let your child know that it may be harder for him to do as well as he did last year, but that you know he is able to make this greater effort. If you focus your attention on his efforts rather than on his grades, you will be supporting his actual work. While I don't like to see children penalized because of the personality characteristics of adults, I believe that it is important for them to learn how to contend with difficult situations.

TEASING
(SEE ALSO *Sibling*)

Some parents express their affection for their children by teasing them in a joking manner. Most children can sense when their parents mean to be affectionate and they are generally not hurt or upset by those remarks unless the remarks are about a particularly embarrassing subject. For instance, a child concerned about being overweight would hardly find it funny to be called "fatty." In such a case, this kind of teasing is downright hostile.

Children vary in their reaction to teasing and parents are usually sensitive enough to their child's reactions to know whether the joking is hurting or demoralizing the child. But if you have any question in your mind as to how your child is taking it, explain to her that you say these things as a joke with no intention of hurting her. Tell her if she prefers not to be teased you will stop.

When children tease one another it can be especially cruel, making a child feel insecure and unhappy. Sibling rivalry often results in malicious teasing; if this occurs it is time for you to intervene. You should make it clear that this kind of behavior is unacceptable. Ask the child how *she* would feel if she were the one being ridiculed. Unless the teasing child has some problems of her own, she will eventually develop sympathy for other people's feelings.

TEETHING
(SEE ALSO *Reassurance, Suffering*)

Not all babies cut their first teeth at the same time—but the average child will get his around six months. He may drool, bite, and fret for three or four months before that. It is not unusual for a three-month-old to have his first tooth; in fact, some babies are even born with a tooth.

Infants will cut twenty teeth during their first two-and-a-half years, sometimes fretting all the while. Children sometimes have fevers accompanying teething, which may occasionally cause parents to think that the child has a cold instead.

When babies teethe, they show a strong need to mouth objects. They bite things and drool a great deal. They are irritable, and frequently wake during the night with a startling, sharp cry. It's as if they have a piercing pain, which causes them to cry out. When this happens it is perplexing to a parent, particularly because the child doesn't seem to awaken completely. He cries out, yet still seems to be asleep. Massaging the baby's gums with your fingers helps, as does having a teething ring or other teething object that has been kept cold.

Teething is very painful and upsetting to a baby. He doesn't understand what's happening and therefore requires more holding and cuddling. Parents sometimes find that a baby who has finally gotten to sleep through the night begins to awake suddenly and often around four to six months of age. This changed pattern is most likely due to the pain caused by teething. When it happens, as inconvenient as it may be, offer reassurance.

TELEVISION, EFFECTS OF
(SEE ALSO *Aggression, Family, Listening, Video Games*)

Parents often want to know how television can affect a child's development. Mothers and fathers are usually most concerned about the violence on TV, and the increasingly open discussion of the horrors of nuclear war, the Holocaust, and graphic accounts of rising crime. I would like to offer some guidelines, and then address the issue of "how much television watching is too much."

I do believe that children should be discouraged from watching violence on television and should instead be encouraged to view more educational programs. Television violence can be harmful to young children. Children can become hard-hearted from watching violence on television. They can also become frightened, worried, or suspicious. Researchers found, too, that children who watch many violent programs tended to be more aggressive on the playground and in the classroom.

One psychologist has formulated a list of actions you can take to help alleviate this potential problem: (1) Watch at least one episode of each program your child watches, so that you know just how violent it is; (2) when you and your child are viewing TV together, discuss the violence with your child; talk about why the violence happens and how painful it was; ask your child for ideas about why the conflict could have been resolved without violence; (3) explain to your child how the violence on entertainment programs is "faked" and what might happen if people actually did such things to one another; (4) encourage your child to watch programs with characters who cooperate well and care for each other; such programs have been shown to influence children in positive ways.

While there are indications that children who see a lot of violence on television will be affected by it, I think it is safe to say that children who pick up a violent or dangerous idea from TV and act on it are probably prone to expressions of violence in the first place; TV reinforced the existing impulse. The initial impulse comes when children live in an atmosphere where adult tempers have short fuses and parents often yell and fight. I should note that violent fairy tales and even biblical stories have been recounted to children for many years without harmful effects.

Of course, some children should be discouraged from watching any violent programs. Some youngsters are more sensitive than others, some may have emotional problems, or extreme fears. It is up to the parent to decide how much each child can handle.

Sometimes, the television is a convenient babysitter. Children watch it passively for hours and some parents even encourage this as a way to keep the children quiet and out of the way. I don't believe that parents should allow such indiscriminate television watching; I think it is too limited in terms of intellectual and emotional stimulation. Parents ought to encourage their children to engage in reading, creative play, musical and sports activities. I can understand that parents need "mini-vacations" from their children and might be inclined to suggest that the children "go watch TV." But television is just one of many possible diversions. If children become addicted to TV, they may make a great fuss later on when parents attempt to cut down on viewing time.

TEMPER TANTRUMS
(SEE ALSO *Aggression, Anger, Arguments Between Parents, Neurological Disturbance*)

Children learn to respond to anger as their parents do. If they observe their parents indulging in histrionics or in angry outbursts, they are likely to exhibit these behaviors themselves.

Parents should, through their own behavior, encourage children to express their negative feelings and frustrations in words, and to seek solutions to the problems underlying these feelings, rather than losing control and screaming, swearing, and throwing things.

Temper trantrums are relatively common among two-year-olds, four-year-olds, and teenagers, however, and the best way to deal with these normal sorts of problems for these developmental stages is to ignore them. Simply walk away and fail to give your child any attention when he is behaving in this way. Of course, this works most effectively when you are at home alone with your child. If you are in someone else's home or in a public place, and your child throws a screaming fit, you may have to restrain him and as quickly as possible move him to a quiet and private place. There you can sit down and hold your child until he regains his composure. You might reassure him by saying calmly, "I know you are angry, and that must feel bad; I'm sorry you feel so bad." Then you can explain that you cannot allow your child to behave in such a way, no matter how bad he feels. Later when your child is back to normal you can discuss with him what happened, including how he made you feel— that is, embarrassed or angry. Reassure your child again that you love him and that you are confident that he can overcome his problem.

You can help your child by encouraging him to release his emotions in other, more acceptable ways, especially by using words to tell what he is feeling, and by trying to solve the problem that is making him so frustrated or angry in the first place. And of course, the best way for him to learn how to handle anger constructively and positively is through your example. If you express your negative feelings, and then work hard to solve the difficulties that caused those feelings, your child will learn to do so too.

TERMINAL ILLNESS, OF A CHILD OR PARENT
(SEE ALSO *Death; Funerals, Taking Children To; Hospitalization; Stuttering*)

I don't believe that any child can cope effectively with the knowledge of his impending death. In fact, in many cases, I don't think a parent can say with complete certainty that a child is going to die— that is, that he will die soon. Doctors try to keep terminally ill children alive as long as possible with the hope that some new medical technique or knowledge may save the child's life. What I am saying is that a child is entitled to hope, even if it is very faint.

I think it is fair to answer your child's questions about his illness and if he expresses the fear that he may die you can say, "Yes, you are ill and it is serious. But everyone is working very hard to make you better so that you can come home soon."

In helping to care for terminally ill children I advise doctors, nurses, and parents to engage the child in projects that have a future —something the child can work on today, tomorrow, and the next day. This helps the child look to the future. Quite unconsciously, many parents stop talking to their child about his future, especially if the youngster's chronic illness will prevent him from reaching adulthood.

Another tendency to be avoided is to become indulgent with a child who is terminally ill. Parents, doctors, and nurses have a tendency to stop enforcing the rules and regulations of daily life and treat him in a way that is inconsistent with the past. This is understandable in light of adult emotions, but it is unfair to the child. It disrupts his life at a time when a return to normalcy would be welcome.

I mentioned that a terminally ill child is entitled to hope. This is true in the case of a terminally ill parent as well. I do believe it is important for children to know whether a parent is seriously ill; it would be not only impossible but dishonest to conceal such information from them. You can explain that while the doctors do not expect Daddy to live for a long time, no one knows for sure just how long he will live.

If you can foster an atmosphere of openness in which everyone can discuss his or her feelings, you will be doing a great service to your children. They should know that it is understandable for them to feel fear or sadness.

In such situations some people try to urge everyone to "be brave" and "put on a smile." This attitude, while well-intended, can make children feel weak or guilty if they cry or express grief. It is right and natural to experience such emotions at a time like this; you should teach your children that to cry does not mean they are weak, but that it is an appropriate way to express deep emotion.

THUMBSUCKING
(SEE ALSO *Infancy, Pacifier, Sucking, Weaning*)

When an infant sucks his thumb it is probably due to his having touched his hand to his face by chance, which served to stimulate the rooting reflex, causing him to move his mouth to whatever is touching his face. This inborn reflex continues for the first four to six months of life, and helps an infant automatically turn to its mother's breast or a bottle, and begin sucking.

When he is put in his crib at bedtime, his hand or thumb may be inadvertently placed near his mouth and he will spontaneously begin to suck. His sucking response provides some gratification that serves to reinforce the pattern and may increase the likelihood that he will suck his thumb again.

There is nothing wrong with this, and it will not interfere with your child's development. If you gently take your baby's hand from his mouth after he goes to sleep he may be less inclined to suck his thumb. If you stay with him, rock him, and hold him as he goes to sleep, it will help him relax without sucking his thumb.

When the sucking need is not gratified in infancy, perhaps as a result of a rigid feeding schedule or because he was not given sufficient sucking time during feeding, he may continue to suck his thumb well beyond his toddler years. Many children will suck their thumbs when tired or under some emotional stress. As time goes by, this gradually diminishes.

Thumbsucking can persist even if a child is emotionally secure because the behavior has simply become a habit. This is not harmful but many parents are bothered by it and feel they must do something. I am totally against teasing or nagging a child or putting iodine or any other bitter material on his thumb to stop thumbsucking. Such humiliating and severe punishment can cause psychological damage that is far worse than the possible dental deformities caused by thumbsucking. My advice is not to make an issue of thumbsucking.

TOILET TRAINING
(SEE ALSO *Bedwetting, Behavior Modification, Discipline and Punishment, Messiness, Soiling*)

It is important for you to view the toilet training process as an opportunity for your child to begin to master his body and control his behavior. Your job as a parent is to help him achieve this by using his own resources. Coercion, punishment, and intense emotions on your part can only have negative consequences.

A child is not physically ready for toilet training until approximately eighteen months of age. Prior to this time, his nervous system is not sufficiently developed.

You should approach his training with an understanding attitude and endless patience, while continuing to promote his independent ability to control his toilet functions. If he sees that you are overly concerned and show extreme joy or anger about where and when he deposits his feces, he will then be able to use toilet habits to please or show annoyance toward you. His feces then become valuable as a source of emotional expression and control over you. Your child feels, "Why would anyone show such concern over something if it weren't so important?" In extreme cases, children may retain their feces and do so by actively withholding them in their bodies. This sometimes requires medical intervention if it goes beyond a few days. It doesn't usually occur unless parents have overemphasized the importance of doing the "right" thing, in the "right" place, at the "right" time! You should express interest in a child's toilet training, but the intensity of your concern should not be so great as to be interpreted by your child as the equivalent of love or loss of love.

You can begin when your child is between two and three years old by letting him know that going to the toilet is expected of him. Adopt a patient, matter-of-fact attitude about your expectations. Even after training has been successful, there will be occasional regressions, particularly if the child is under some pressure or stress. Perhaps the most frequent cause of regression is the birth of a sibling shortly after a child has been toilet trained. Quite understandably parents want to avoid the difficulties of caring for two children in diapers at the same time, but rushing toilet training when a new child is expected more often than not causes problems when the sibling is born. No self-respecting child will give up diapers when the new intruder is given all kinds of love and attention while being cared for and diapered! It is normal for children around two years old to be negativistic and at times defiant, which is all the more reason for not making toilet training a battle between you and your child.

Another problem is that if you stress toilet training too early, and with too much intensity, your child may begin to feel that only neatness, cleanliness, and orderliness will invariably lead to the most positive parental responses. After all, you seem so pleased. The child develops a connection between a ritual of neatness and parental acceptance and love.

It's not uncommon for a child to become frightened of the toilet when he is sitting on it and it's flushed. Little children are fearful that they themselves can actually be flushed down the toilet. This kind of fear is normal, and should be respected, so avoid flushing the toilet until after your child is finished. In fact, it's best to let the child do the flushing himself. Don't be surprised if he waves "bye-bye" to what was once part of his body. This is one more step in a process of a child's mastery of his own bodily functions.

It is also not unusual for children, who are curious about everything at the age of two or three, to want to touch their feces. They view it as their "own product" and don't think of feces as bad, ugly, or disgusting so they want to explore. I think it is all right to allow your child to touch his feces, maybe in the bathtub, and to inspect them. Once the child has satisfied his curiosity, his inquisitiveness will end.

In general, you should avoid associating the products of toilet functions with feelings of disgust or distaste. A matter-of-fact attitude is better. If your attitude is prohibitive, it may increase his fascination and desire to play with his feces. You may also lead your child to believe that the genital area is "dirty" or "disgusting," which can interfere with a healthy sexual development. On the other hand, if you offer encouragement, your child may place greater emphasis on his feces than necessary. There was a time when child care experts encouraged parents to allow their children to play with their feces to avoid interfering with "developing creativity." I'm glad that day has passed.

TRAVEL
(SEE ALSO *Babysitter, Depression, Separation Anxiety, Summer Camp*)

The humorist Robert Benchley once wrote that there were two classes of travel—first class, and with children. Nevertheless, I think it is a good idea for parents to take children, even infants, on vacation trips. I realize that many people would like to be able to get away from young children totally for a week or two. Unfortunately, this can cause ill effects. It is possible that on your return your child will ignore you, or perhaps he will have regressed in his behavior. He may even have been depressed and refused to eat while you were gone. These are the normal, understandable reactions of a baby who truly wants and needs his parents. Ideally, you should wait to take trips away from your baby until he can talk and can understand time well enough for him to comprehend "now," "later," and "tomorrow." This is usually possible when the child is close to three years old.

If you take your youngster on a trip, he will become accustomed to new places and new situations in the sheltering presence of his parents, who provide the security he needs to adjust to new environments. When traveling with children, try to find out in advance whether they will be readily accommodated. If you are going on a plane, particularly if it is a long flight, it's advisable to inform the airline that you will be taking a baby aboard. Sometimes special treatment is provided that makes the trip easier.

As far as airplane travel is concerned, adults know that when aircraft take off and land, the cabin pressure changes. We have learned to swallow or open our mouths to make our ears "pop." But babies do not know these tricks, so you need to help by giving your baby something to suck on while the plane is changing altitude. When a baby screams on an airplane, it is probably because the change in pressure is causing pain in his ears.

TWINS AND OTHER MULTIPLES
(SEE ALSO *Sibling*)

The psychological problems that twins and other multiples may develop are basically no different from the psychological problems that any child may develop. The major concern I have about twins centers on the fact that children require a great deal of time and attention, and when you have twins it is difficult to give each of them the time and attention that you would have been able to give a single child. Rearing twins obviously takes more time and requires more energy and ingenuity on the part of the parents. This does not necessarily make twins more vulnerable to problems, but it certainly makes your task as a parent more demanding. By the same token, though, I am sure your joys and pleasures are increased simply because you have two children rather than one to provide you with parental satisfaction.

It is very common for parents to treat twins as a unit. Feeding them the same and entertaining them with the same games and toys is probably a good idea, since their developmental needs are probably quite similar. If, however, you find that one twin enjoys a particular kind of attention or recreation, I would certainly respect that need and adapt an individual program for her as much as possible without giving in to unreasonable demands. Twins should be thought of and dealt with not as a unit but as two separate human beings—even if they both want the same things.

There are a number of problems that many parents of twins encounter to some extent. Twins sometimes gang up on their parents. Also, sometimes one parent prefers one twin, and the other parent may respond by picking the other twin to be his or her favorite. Sometimes which twin is older and which younger—even if only by thirty seconds—may become an issue. Sometimes twins develop their own words, and even their own language. Sometimes other siblings may suffer from being constantly compared to twins. But problems like these can be talked out within the family. What is important is that twins be regarded as individuals.

By the way, when you prepare your other children for the birth of multiple siblings, you needn't assume that the event will be particularly confusing or even traumatic to them. Most little children have been exposed to some animal—usually a cat, dog, hamster, or pet mouse. These animals all have multiple births, so more than one baby does not seem all that unusual to children. Even if they have not been exposed to animals, children are generally not as surprised by multiple births as are adults.

V

VIDEO GAMES
(SEE ALSO *Television, Effects of*)

There is no problem inherent in video games. Video games in and of themselves are harmless. In fact, they can be a positive experience. They can be very challenging intellectually as well as challenging to physical coordination. Many children—and adults, for that matter—are fascinated with them. I hasten to point out that while some of them have a war-like theme that involves shooting down enemies, others have objectives that are non-military and non-aggressive. It is the latter that are completely non-objectionable in my view.

When parents find themselves discussing the problem of video games, they need to determine exactly what problem they're talking about. The major controversy when video games were first introduced had to do with ancillary activities at video-game parlors. Parents found their children spending large amounts of money, having contact with drug pushers, and inclined to be more influenced by peer pressure to defy parents. It was the environment in which video games were presented that was the problem, not the video games themselves.

Now that video games can be found inside many homes, children can play them there, with other family members. It would seem that the major problem now might be teaching children how to limit the time they spend playing video games, as opposed to playing outdoors or doing their homework or helping with household chores. This seems to me a problem that parents and children can solve together, in the same way that they have solved the problems of how much time can be spent listening to the radio or records or watching TV.

I would not advise that parents ban their children's participation in video game playing. It seems to be generally true that when something is prohibited it becomes more fascinating than when it is tolerated. There also seems to be a general tendency for human beings to react with horror at any innovation that threatens the status quo. Certainly radio raised some furor until it became integrated into life, and TV did the same. I have a great deal of faith in human fortitude, and I feel certain that parents and children together can master the problem of integrating video games into their lives.

W

WEANING
(SEE ALSO *Breastfeeding, Infancy, Sucking*)

Because of individual differences, some babies can be weaned from the breast or bottle when they are close to one year of age, but most babies require a bottle until they are three, and in some instances, even older. Such circumstances as illness, stress in the family, or the birth of a sibling, may increase a baby's desire to continue sucking.

Many pediatricians recommend weaning a child around the time he begins to teethe. In my opinion, teething is not a good indicator, since the presence of teeth does not affect a baby's need for sucking. Moreover, most babies begin to get teeth around six to eight months, which is far too soon to begin weaning a baby.

A primary task for a baby in the first year of life is to develop a sense of trust. This can best be accomplished when parents are responsive to a baby's needs, and the need for sucking satisfaction is an important one. So don't try to wean him in his first year; wait until he is in his second year, and begin slowly, while you're teaching your child to feed himself.

Ideally, you should show your child how to use a cup sometime between four to six months of age. Do this while your child is still being breast- or bottle-fed. In this way you will be teaching your child two different ways of taking food. If you allow your child the sucking gratification of feeding from the breast or bottle while he learns to drink from a cup, the weaning will be less stressful. The parent who decides that at a predetermined time his child must give up the nipple and take on the difficult task of drinking from a cup will only encounter problems. If the weaning process itself becomes very stressful, the desire for sucking gratification increases and a vicious cycle is set in motion.

The most successful techniques allow the child who can feed himself to continue to have a bottle or the breast at some time during the day, which usually turns out to be bedtime. Generally speaking, it is much easier for your child to give up sucking during the day than to give it up when he needs to suck to relax and go off to sleep at night. Eventually, when you stop even the bedtime bottle, your child may want you to spend more time holding, rocking, and cuddling him. There is nothing wrong with doing this, since it serves to help him outgrow his need to suck as a means of relaxation.

If you try to wean your child before he is ready, you will intensify his frustration and also intensify his need for sucking gratification. Some mothers put off weaning because they may enjoy the child's dependency. If the mother is inclined to encourage and reward that dependency, it can interfere with the child's emotional development. But weaning your child too late is generally not as detrimental as doing it too soon.

WHINING

The child who whines endlessly about little things has been encouraged to do so—often by the very adults who find this behavior so upsetting. I am convinced that the child who whines has had to rely on whining to get attention. This child's parents didn't answer her cries—or they didn't answer her cries until she began to whine. Such parents may be concerned about "spoiling" their child by giving her attention as soon as she cries, and may instead wait until the child begins to cry continually or to whine. Whining becomes her only means to get attention.

If your child whines, I recommend that you respond by saying emphatically, "I do not understand you when you whine, and I will not be able to listen to you until you stop your whining and speak clearly." In that way you are being responsive to your child and her needs, while at the same time discouraging the whining.

WITHDRAWN CHILD
(SEE ALSO *Adolescence, Anger, Arguments Between Parents, Autism, Bashfulness, Daydreaming, Model Child, Moving, Neurological Disturbances, Neurosis, Schizophrenia, Shyness*)

The quiet, obedient child who is no trouble to anyone, but who smiles very little and appears to lack the ability to have fun may be a withdrawn child who engages in fantasies that are more satisfying to him than the real world. Unfortunately, many of these "good, well-behaved" children are in real trouble. They are apt to come apart later in life, particularly during adolescence, when the pressures of life may seem overwhelming. In the life of such a child there is a lot of undischarged hostility building up. At some point along the way the child got the message from his parents that anger was bad, but he was not taught how to channel his negative feelings appropriately in a constructive manner.

If your child seems withdrawn, the first thing you might do is rule out the possibility that he is suffering from some physiological disturbance such as a metabolic disorder or nervous system dysfunction. You will need the help of a pediatrician and possibly a neurologist to make this determination.

Often childhood emotional problems occur because of some family problems such as parental arguments. Moving from place to place or changing schools can also disrupt a child's life; sometimes if he has not been adequately prepared he may have trouble adjusting and making new friends. Perhaps the child has been terrorized by another youngster, a school bully, and has been so frightened he can't bring himself to tell you. There are any number of traumatic events in a child's life, and I needn't list them all here. If you are unable to uncover the source of the problem, I strongly urge you to consult a professional.

Sometimes a child becomes withdrawn and alienated from his

family because he feels he cannot live up to his parents' expectations. Some parents, without realizing it, may instill feelings of rejection or "not being good enough" by holding up standards their child cannot possibly accomplish. This can cause a child to make what seems the best possible adjustment, which is isolating himself from people, engaging in an active fantasy life, and disregarding the real world. Not infrequently we read about such youngsters who have committed destructive acts against society or who act out their fantasies without realizing the difference between fantasy and reality. Such children need help.

While some youngsters who withdraw may be emotionally troubled, I suspect that many teenagers who retreat are often simply struggling to assert themselves and establish their independence. Adolescents are often experimenting with different ideas and philosophies and they fantasize about the future. Sometimes these fantasies mean withdrawing into his own room, shutting the door, and listening to music for hours. If this sounds like your teenager, I don't think there is a need for a great deal of concern, as long as he shows no signs of depression, distress, or bizarre behavior. If he does seem depressed and under pressure, you might want to consult a psychologist who specializes in counseling adolescents. This will give your child a chance to talk to someone outside the family. In this way you can offer help and reassure yourself at the same time that there are no underlying emotional disorders.

INDEX

225